FROM INCOGNITO GANGSTER TO GOD—

*An American
Story of
Redemption and
Restoration*

A Memoir

TOM POPE

Published By:
Tom Pope Media, LLC
Washington, D.C.
Email: Tom@tompopemedia.com
Website: Tompopemedia.com

Packaging/Consulting Services
Professional Publishing House
1425 W. Manchester Ave. Ste. B
Los Angeles, California 90047
323-750-3592
Email:.professionalpublishinghouse@yahoo.com
www.Professionalpublishinghouse.com

Cover design: TWASolutions
First printing November 2018
ISBN: 978-0-578-40750-0
10987654321

Dedication

I dedicate this book to God, my wife, Gwen, son and daughter, Thomas and Terie, my father and mother, my grandparents, my siblings, my pastors, my publisher, my friends, my mentors, and all the persons who played a pivotal role in making me the man I am today.

I want to extend a special dedication to my mother, Artelia Pope Belle, who transitioned to be with the Lord, during the editing, and just prior to the publication, of this book. Although my heart is broken now with the loss of both of my parents, their strength has given me the courage to press on and honor them by fulfilling God's plan for my life!

Contents

Contents

Contents

***Gospel of Matthew Chapters 1-28—First book of the New
Testament.***
***The Genealogy of Christ, His Ministry, Rejection by Israel and
His Gift to the Whole World.***

INTRODUCTION

"O Israel, hope in the Lord; for with the Lord there is mercy, and with Him is abundant redemption."

– Psalm 130:7-8

Incognito—means having one's authentic identity concealed, or an assumed, or false identity.

synonyms: under an assumed name, under a false name, in disguise, under cover, in plain clothes, camouflaged or unidentified.

Alpha Male—the dominant male animal in a particular group. A man tending to assume a dominant or domineering role in social or professional situations.

Alpha Male Popular Urban Term—the "alpha male" is a real man, is a man's man, a warrior, a stand-up guy. It doesn't matter what you call him, he's a leader; the guy who others look to for motivation, inspiration, and often with a hint of jealousy.

---

*F*rom Incognito Gangster to God: An American Story of Redemption and Restoration is my personal story and testament to the awesome power of God! It's about how He could change the heart of an angry and bitter young man who was sliding down a path of death and destruction. Yet through Divine Intervention, God turned around what was meant for evil into a transformed life of good that glorifies Him. I'm a living witness that God can use anybody for His purpose! I've also asked those I could physically reach, or who are now reading this book, to forgive me for my past transgressions, too.

This book also debunks the myth that Blacks don't experience the nuclear family of having both a father and mother in the same home. God placed the best character traits of my parents into me. I am the beneficiary of my father's wit, analytical mind, physical and mental toughness and humor.

Mom, Dad, Grandma Esther, June, Kenny and me

George and me in cowboy and soldier outfits.

My mother deposited her creativity, tenacity, focus, love of reading and education into me. Both of my parents pursued education later in life and were talkers with exceptional speaking skills. No small wonder that I became a broadcaster, writer, media marketing specialist, political strategist and an athlete.

This literary effort is not meant to be a ***How-to-Book on Crime*** that extols criminal activity. Rather, it is a book that will help its reader recognize and draw on positive and negative life experiences in their personal quest to find themselves in Christ. I hope this book will literally scare the "hell" out of you, once you realize the extent of evil that is seeking to devour you at a moment's notice.

Flattery is one of the primary tools Satan uses to ensnare those who crave power. These victims are usually greedy, gullible, shallow, or insecure. They think they're smarter than everybody else. Satan also seeks out those who are lonely and crave attention, filling their perceived void with sweet things they want to hear and feel.

Sadly, they find out much too late that sweet ain't sweet. Generally, they will have lost what they once had. I was a crafty predator who skillfully employed these tactics on my prey, not caring about whom, or what, I destroyed. I will elaborate on these themes in later chapters of my book, *From Incognito Gangster to God: An American Story of Redemption and Restoration.*

At the end of each chapter, I have included a **Lessons Learned and Thoughts to Ponder** section. I pray this will be useful to you as a tool for further contemplation and study.

PROLOGUE

I am an extremely private and introverted person by nature, who was comfortable living out my life based on my current public persona and reputation. It took the Almighty God to direct me to open myself up to public scrutiny and lay bare my soul for all to see. Please learn from my life experiences and know that God can, and will, use whomsoever He wills to do His work!

From Incognito Gangster to God: An American Story of Redemption and Restoration is a clarion call and an in-your-face type book that will cause reflection on the extent of your faith and the power of Satan! The Devil is a formidable opponent who has a tremendous amount of resources at his disposal. He employs a bag of time-tested tricks. He has layers of demons with varying powers, assignments and an endless number of disciples. (These disciples make un-believers susceptible to being used by the forces of evil to work with him for the sole purpose of turning you from God.)

I personally know how strong Satan is because I was one of his disciples who enjoyed doing his bidding before I woke up in time and returned to following Christ.

Most people don't know who they are, or their history. They are generally living in some form of denial. It's time to stop playing church and being part-time Christians who are not totally committed to God. And if you are an unbeliever in Christ, the Devil has you right where he wants you. That is, sentenced to spend the rest of your life in Hell. Good deeds and being a nice person won't help you escape from living an eternity in Hell with Satan.

Here's my first point providing context for you, the reader, of my book. When I was a babe in Christ, I often skipped reading crucial portions of various books of the Bible because it was boring to me. I could not understand the significance of some names used and why they were even listed. At the time, I didn't know who I was.

The *Book of Matthew, Chapter 1:1-17,* was a glaring example of my naivety. It was years later before I understood the relevance of knowing your history, forefathers, and genealogy. I came to understand the impact of the forefathers' very being and the decisions they made, which affected my life, causing generational blessings, or curses, to fall upon me. Genesis 17:7 assures us that God's covenants, grace and mercy, for those who love Him and keep His commandments covers their children and future generations.

Conversely, those who reject Him and who sin, God's judgments fall on them until the third and fourth generations. (Deuteronomy 5:9-10).

The second contextual point for my book is the word, **Dispensation**. In Christian theology, **Dispensation** is a divinely ordained order, or practices, prevailing at a certain period of Christian history. Simply put, God holds you accountable for what you should know at the time of your life. Old Testament saints were judged, or held accountable, to a different standard than that of New Testament saints.

My last point of context deals with the term **Divine Connection**. Regardless of what age group, or generation you are a member of, I trust this term will briefly pull us away from narrow generational thoughts, open our minds and put us all on the same page. Both mine and your ancestors are, and were, products of their times. Ethnicity, period, access to education, or lack thereof, geographical or geopolitical upbringing shaped their perceptions and views of the world in which they lived.

Many of our early ancestors did not have the socio-economic advantages we currently enjoy. Accordingly, they heard and lived by the information and rules of their times. Those ancestors internalized those lessons and some of them prospered because of God's *Divine Connection* with them. Today, some of us are blessed, and not for anything we have done. Rather, we are blessed because of the connection God had with some of our ancestors, and He extended His grace to us because of them. "Judge not, that you be judged. For with what judgement you judge, you will be judged; and the measure you use, it will be measured back to you." (Matthew 7:1-2).

CHAPTER ONE

Humble Beginnings

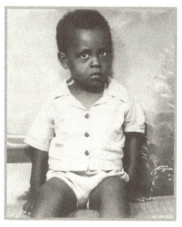

Young me, sitting on a chair.

A Man Who has a Right to be a Leader

Walk with me through the various chapters of my life that will evolve before you. I'm a product of the *Baby Boomer* generation who was born to become an Alpha Male. I was also born Black and "Dirt Poor" in rural southern Kentucky in the year

1948. Back then, times were tough for both Black and White people. My parents went to the "Colored" school, which was separate and un-equal. My mother dropped out of high school, but later in life, gained her high school GED and went on to become a Nurse and Head Start official for Erie County in Ohio.

My father drove past the high school, never graduating from it. Early in life, he turned to a nefarious career of crime, specializing in bootlegging, moonshining, cattle rustling, gambling and was in and out of jail for a variety of offenses. Later in life, he became a Millwright for the Aluminum & Magnesium Plant in Sandusky, Ohio. My father, although lacking a formal education, taught himself how to read and write. He made me read the newspaper with him daily. This is something I regularly do to this day.

One of the most impactful moments of my life was when my father, who was studying to become a Millwright, told me he couldn't read or write that well. Thus, he asked me to help him with his homework. Together, we passed all the written tests he had to take, and he eventually became a Millwright. I learned from my father to never be too proud to ask for help!

Financially, my parents were not doing well during my infancy, at the time we lived in Kentucky. Their only saving grace was my grandmother's (my mother's mother) farm that sustained all of us. My grandmother, Esther, and her brother, Uncle Pete, co-owned the farm. Together they raised cattle, hogs, chickens and planted crops. My grandmother was an astute businesswoman who sold her products directly to the local stores and neighbors in her area. She was also a seamstress on the side. She taught my mother how to sew, which led her to become a master seamstress, too.

Grandma Esther & Mr. Willie on their farm

Experiencing Racism First-Hand has a Long-Lasting Impact

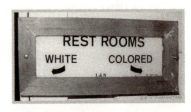

In later years, (1950s and early 1960s), my sister, June, middle brother, George, and I were shipped from Ohio in the North, down to Kentucky in the South, to spend each summer with my grandparents. This was the first time I came face-to-face with systemic, overt racism. In the North, racism was subtle. On the drive down, my mother would always pack boxes of sandwiches, chicken and sweets we would eat in parks along the way. We would use the restrooms there. I looked forward to those picnics! When we stopped at gas stations, it was only to purchase gas, or buy pops (sodas).

Years later, I found out why we had all those picnics. It was because we weren't allowed to eat in the restaurants, and the only thing you could buy at most gas stations was gasoline. A lot of them didn't want you using their restrooms, either. While in the South, I read the "White Only" and "Colored" signs displayed just about anywhere Black and White people intersected, especially at drinking fountains, restrooms, restaurants and movie theatres (Blacks had to sit in the balcony). I became angry and wanted to strike back at an early age, however, my grandmother tempered my anger.

"Baby, we have to live here with these people after you go back north," she would say.

I thought she was weak at the time, but I would go onto learn just how strong she and my grandfather were in terms of how they lived their productive lives under the sweltering grip of racial oppression and open, state-sanctioned discrimination.

Entrepreneurism is a Means to Level the Economic Playing Field and Gain Prosperity

In my frequent future trips, south to Kentucky, I would better understand my grandmother's entrepreneurial spirit that she passed onto me. It was through entrepreneurship that she gained her economic freedom while in the grips of sweltering, extreme racism. As the scripture points out, God will prepare a table before you in the presence of your enemies. (Psalm 23:5).

*Grandmother Esther sitting on the
side of her bed.*

During those summers my grandmother taught me so much about life in my youth that those lessons are now permanently ingrained in my DNA. She taught me how to conduct business as she sold her goods to both Black and White people. Plus, she drilled into me that I must own my own land. And she told me **NOT** to ever let anybody take my land, or anything else from me. She was surrounded by a sea of White people, some of whom were good, but most of who were extremely mean. These Whites vehemently resented the fact that she owned her own land and was prosperous, too.

Always Protect Yourself!

Grandma Esther, whom I called "Momma Etchin," due to my speech impediment because I couldn't pronounce Esther at the time, taught me how to shoot a pistol. This was my first introduction to gun ownership. I learned how to accurately hit what I was shooting at. We all know that Malcom X popularized the phrase, "***Send um to the cemetery!***" "Momma Etchin," who stood all of 4 foot, 6 inches tall, was known to shoot at people, if they came onto her land, uninvited. Way back then, she lived in her own gated-community. To her, "No Trespassing" meant "Come onto my land uninvited at your own peril." To underscore and enforce this belief, she kept a large pack of snarling, barking dogs for alerting her of an outsider's presence. "Momma Etchin" deposited her combative, sometimes mean spirit, into me. I also learned from her that if people know you are willing and able to defend yourself, but they are still silly enough to gore your ox, they know retribution is imminent, and you will swiftly kill their cow.

The Ku Klux Klan was active in her community and routinely terrorized Black people. However, the racists left my people alone because they showed no fear, were vigilant and would not back down when confronted by evil, especially while on their own land that was fortified by a pack of vicious dogs and plenty of loaded pistols, rifles and shotguns they knew how to use. If you resist the Devil, he will soon flee. (James 4:7).

The other part of my summer visits with "Mama Etchin" that resonated with me, was spending time with her husband, whom we affectionately called Mr. Willie. Mr. Willie was a man small of stature who regularly carried a concealed pistol. He and "Mama Etchin" were equally yoked. Mr. Willie helped me perfect my marksmanship with small arms. Whenever a huge turtle would foolishly come out of the nearby river and walk across the yard, he would shoot, skin and cook it.

Mr. Willie also instilled a love of radio programming into me. This was a time when a radio was a major piece of furniture in a person's living room. In the evenings during the Golden Age of Radio, which began in the early1920s and lasted until the 1950s, we, like other families, would gather around the radio and listen to programs such as (*Gunsmoke, Amos 'n' Andy, Red Skelton, Music* and *News*

programs) that, as an infant, captured my imagination.

We would make ice cream, and I would roll my grandfather's tobacco into cigarettes for him. When I got older, rolling weed (marijuana) was second nature to me, based on the skillset I learned rolling cigarettes as a youth. I told Mr. Willie when

I was about 5 years old that I wanted to go into radio, and he told me I could do anything I wanted to do, if I worked hard enough at it. Also, while I was a baby and then a toddler, my mother would lay me on a blanket in front of the radio and I would sit there all day fascinated by what I heard. I often asked myself, at the time, *how did all those voices get inside of that small box?* I wanted to join them.

Lessons Learned and Thoughts to Ponder:

1. Know your history.

2. Never be too proud to ask for help.

3. Own some property and land.

4. Eat natural food that you grow.

5. God will prepare a table before you in the presence of your enemies. (Psalm 23:5).

6. Racism is real—even today; don't be lulled into a false sense of thinking it's gone.

7. Have (within the law) and know how to shoot a gun—even in today's climate of doing away with firearms.

8. Have positive people sow into your life on a regular basis and always resist voices of negativity.

9. If you resist the Devil, he will soon flee. (James 4:7).

10. Find your passion and regularly pursue it.

11. Get an education - reading people are ruling people.

12. Ask God for a good spouse and then get along with them.

CHAPTER TWO

Formative Years, 1948-1967

Hidden Inside Your Adversities are the Keys to Opportunities and Success

In rural southern Kentucky, my father worked odd jobs. He was also heavily involved in bootlegging, gambling, cattle rustling and an assortment of other crimes. He was routinely in and out of jail for minor offenses and committed some serious crimes that could not be proven. The police told him he had two choices. One, get out of Kentucky, and leave the state immediately or two, face serious jail time. My parents' hastened departure from Kentucky, under threat of incarceration of my father, opened the door for a better education and opportunities in the North for all of us.

In 1950, my parents literally ran for the border, taking us on a journey to Ohio's 3 Cs, Cincinnati, Columbus and Cleveland, eventually settling in Sandusky, Ohio. This is the route many in my family took, migrating to better jobs and opportunities in the North because we had relatives residing in those cities that you could live with until you economically got on your feet.

Sandusky, Ohio, 1950

Me in a stroller

We eventually settled into predominately white-populated Sandusky, Ohio. Sandusky is, and was, a town with a large Italian and Jewish community, also containing a significant number of whites from East European countries as well as from West Virginia, Kentucky and Indiana. Blacks comprised less than 10% of the population when my family arrived.

Sandusky's economy at the time was based on heavy and light manufacturing, steel and aluminum producing plants, ball bearing plants, and a Ford assembly plant coupled with industries and manufacturers who supported the automotive industry. You could get a decent paying job, if you wanted to work.

Regardless what side of town you lived on in Sandusky, the schools were great and children received a good education. My family was now not "Dirt Poor;" however, we were still poor. In retrospect, I now realize this was another time where God intervened into the course of my life. We moved to what is called East Parish Street, which is a street with neighboring streets on either side of it. The way this portion of the school district was drawn, at the time, mandated that all the students who lived on East Parish, who were mostly black, except for five white families, went to Hancock Elementary School where all the rich white kids attended. Blacks and a few Whites on the other two streets went to Ontario Elementary School, which was good, but an inferior school.

Hancock Elementary School, Sandusky, Ohio

Ontario Elementary School, Sandusky, Ohio

I received a superior educational foundation, learned a foreign language in grade school and became a star athlete, excelling in baseball, football, basketball and track. My first-grade teacher, Ms. Wilnue, told me I had the ability to write. She mentored and encouraged me through grade school to become a writer since I stuttered so badly. I credit

Ms. Wilnue and my mother for instilling the love of books and reading in me. Meantime, some of my other teachers hated me (because I was Black) and did not want me in their classrooms. My German Language teacher, who also taught History, despised me. She was blatant in her disdain towards me. I could never attain higher than a "C" in any of her classes, despite being an outstanding student in all my other classes.

Nevertheless, at a young age, I became a voracious reader. In addition to reading comic books like any other kid, I also read classic books, too. My mother bought us a set of Britannica Encyclopedia books and strongly encouraged us to read them, further fueling my pursuit of intellectual knowledge. She also regularly took me to the public library and got me my own library card. Having my own library card was important to me. It meant I could unlock the mysteries of a world outside of my personal life and gain knowledge. Through my newspaper route, I envisioned myself as a businessman. So one of the first books I read was *Ragged Dick* by Horatio Alger. This was a story, about a poor bootblack's (shoe shine boy) rise to middle-class respectability. This was something I felt destined to achieve. Horatio Alger resonated with me because he was a prolific writer. He is best known for his many young adult novels about impoverished boys and their rise from humble backgrounds to lives of middle-class security and comfort through hard work, determination, courage and honesty. His writings were characterized by a "rags-to-riches" storyline that was right up my alley. I also read seminal books by the Greek Philosopher, Homer, like *The Odyssey* and *The Iliad*; *The Prince* by Italian Statesman Niccolò Machiavelli, father of modern political theory; and the American classic book *Huckleberry Finn* by Mark Twain. Over the years, I would re-read these works numerous times and apply lessons learned into how I dealt with people. My deceptive tactics and wanderlust were honed from content in *The Odyssey* and *The Iliad*.

The art of real-politics and believing the "Ends justify the means" was straight out of *The Prince* by Niccolò Machiavelli is also credited with the following philosophies, which became ingrained in my DNA:

1. It is better to be feared than loved, if you cannot be both.
2. Men judge generally more by the eye than by the hand, for everyone can see and few can feel.
3. Everyone sees what you appear to be; few really know what you are.

Lessons learned especially from *The Prince*, were integral to the success of my *Incognito Gangster* activities as well as my broadcasting and Spin Doctoring (Media Relations) career. I became a devout student of Machiavellianism, which explained my tendency to be unemotional, and therefore, able to easily detach myself from conventional morality. I could deceive and manipulate others with no thought of remorse. Throughout the course of my life, understanding these principles made detecting those traits and larceny in others, easily recognizable. Even in ministry, this knowledge, coupled with God's gift of "Discernment," has helped me sniff out trouble before it could take root.

Cadillac El Dorado in Sandusky, Ohio

Buick Skylark in Sandusky, Ohio

I also learned about Jewish and Italian cultures, in particular, and white people, in general, during my formative years. This is not meant to stereotype these ethnic groups. Black readers of this book understand required coping techniques, regarding survival and social interaction with these ethnic groups. These experiences were an important life-lesson, which taught me how to interact with other cultures and thrive while doing so.

The Jews, who owned most of the businesses at the time, taught me about business ownership and gave me jobs in their businesses. Although not discussed openly, many in the Italian community who lived so-called respectable lives, in reality were involved in organized crime. I spent a great deal of time in their homes and often ate dinner with them. Some of my young Italian friends' fathers mentored me before and during my life of crime. My main Italian mentor told me to, "Get rid of your flashy Cadillac Eldorado" that I had just purchased. He said, "You're drawing too much attention to yourself. Get rid of it **NOW** because it's bad for business!"

I did and bought a conservative 1968 Buick Skylark, which kept me below the radar. To further lower my criminal profile, I opted to be labeled a playboy, rather than a gangster in-training (*Incognito Gangster*). When many of the Italian kids grew up, they went into the family business and did business with me because we grew up together, knew and could trust each other. I was a quasi-made man. Remember, the Devil can, and will, open doors for you and tempt you, too. (Matthew 4:8-11).

Me on my bike with newspaper bag in Sandusky, Ohio

These connections growing up opened a lot of doors for me that were closed to other Black people in Sandusky. After serving an unpaid newspaper boy apprenticeship, I became the first Black boy to have a major newspaper route because people knew and liked me. Back then, newspaper boys had to deliver and collect payment for the papers they sold. So, I learned customer service skills early, such as knowing when my customers got paid, who would pay on time, who wouldn't, and who couldn't keep their bill current which impacted collections and my payment. I extended credit to the elderly, as well as those who were on strike and not receiving a full pay check. I also saved my customers' papers for them when they were on vacation and collected the mail so that things would not pile up on their porches and front doors, which led to my receiving significant tips as a reward for my efforts.

The paper route also taught me how to subcontract. Because I served my customers well, they would ask me to cut their grass in the summer, rake leaves in the fall, shovel snow in the winter and do odd jobs such as clean up garages. I had so much business and money coming in; I started employing my friends to do the work that I couldn't personally handle. I would have my customers pay me then I in turn would pay my workers, taking my cut off the top, after I had inspected the work to see if it was done to my satisfaction. I learned to "trust but verify" before paying people. I also employed my older sister and a younger Black paperboy apprentice, (whom I felt compelled to pay out of my own pocket), to deliver papers when I was too busy. This way I could help another Black guy get ahead, if he was willing to work hard and not mess up my business and reputation. Plus, my mother and father would deliver the papers when I couldn't. At this point, I advised my parents I didn't need to receive an allowance from them anymore and for them to give the money to my sister and brother. I wish you could have seen the expressions on my parents' faces when I made this pronouncement.

Another God moment happened in my life.

Find Your Passion in Life and Doggedly Pursue It!

As stated previously, my grandfather, Mr. Willie, ignited a passion and instilled a love of radio programming into me during the *Golden Age of Radio*. In fact, my entire family loved radio and always had a record player, so music, news and creative programs routinely permeated our household. And my sister, June, was the motivating force when it came to buying records. My grandparents, parents and sister always listened to a 50,000 watt AM radio station out of Nashville, Tennessee, whose call letters were WLAC.

At nighttime, WLAC had an R&B format during the 1950s, 1960s and 1970s. Most people referred to WLAC as Randy's because Randy's Record Shop was the primary sponsor of the R&B formatted-music programming along with Ernie's Record Mart, both out of the Nashville, Tennessee, area. I can still hear the magical voices of DJs Gene Nobles, John R., Herman Gizzard and the legendary Bill *Hossman* Allen! I imitated their deliveries while my sister ordered the hit records they spun and the record packages they sold via mail order. For my younger readers, back then there was no such thing as downloads and mp3 files sent via the Internet.

Nevertheless, I knew I was part of something big because people were listening from all over the country from the Deep South, to Chicago, Detroit, and Cleveland and up to the northeast portion of the country! WLAC described itself as the nighttime station for half the nation! This further inflamed my passion to get into radio and be on the air as a DJ, despite my being a chronic stutterer.

Create Your Own Internship Opportunities and Volunteer Your Time to Gain Access

On my paper route, there was a radio station whose call letters were WLEC-AM. This was the first time I got to look inside of my life's passion, which was and remains, radio. Starting at the age of 9, I would stop for 5-10 minutes each day and just look in the window of the radio station. I would watch the announcers and news reporters work until they would run me away, most times calling me the N-word! This happened, even though I was their paperboy, delivering their newspaper. After being chased away for nearly 2 years, at the ripe old age of 11, I caught a break.

I never will forget what one of the White engineers said to me: "Boy, I'll probably hate myself for doing this, but since you're so damned determined to come in and see what a real radio station is all about, come on in, but don't touch anything, boy!"

I was ecstatic, exhilarated, elated and almost fainted, all at the same time! Now let me show you another demonstration of the awesome power of God who can see into our future and prepare us for opportunities coming our way!

"All things are possible through Christ."

– Philippians 4:13

Most who know me today would never guess I was a former chronic stutterer. All my life I had told my parents I wanted to be a radio announcer. But just like Moses, I was not a good public speaker and stuttered badly and had no Aaron to talk for me. Fortunately for me, my parents didn't tell me I couldn't become a radio announcer or discourage me from pursuing that career. Instead, they scraped together the money when I was about 9 years old and sent me to a speech pathologist that taught me how to speak properly and deal with my chronic stuttering. I must have been a sight, practicing being a newscaster while reading my newspapers and stuttering so badly.

Some of my Black friends ridiculed me for learning how to speak differently and said I was trying to sound white. It hurt me at the time, but I did what I had to do to become an announcer. After two hard years of study and practice, I no longer stuttered. God then opened another door by moving on the heart of the radio station manager to let me do odd jobs around the station, such as emptying trash cans, getting coffee for the announcers and newscasters and clearing the teletype machines of wire copy that I would read and practice reading aloud. I eventually became their copy boy and got the opportunity to regularly get into a studio and practice being an announcer. They told me that some Negroes (current terminology for Blacks at the time) in big cities were on the radio and making a living doing it, too! I said to myself, *I could do that, too!*

One day, a time salesman came into the station with a contract whose spots (commercials) had to air that weekend. The problem was they needed a kid's voice on the radio spot. The salesman, program director and station manager were perplexed about how they could find a kid on such short notice that late in the day. I spoke up in my best white sounding, *"Beaver Cleaver"* voice. "I could do it," I said.

I could sense that deep reservation had set in by all, however, economics drove the deal when the salesman enthusiastically said, "its radio and nobody will see him and know that he's a Negro. Plus, the kid sounds white!"

Done deal. Then I asked, "You guys get paid for doing these commercials so I want to be paid, too."

After what seemed like an hour of hand wringing, the station manager said, "Okay, kid, I'll pay you." That was the beginning of my on-air broadcast career. I had finally gained their respect after delivering when the pressure was on and received high marks for my faithful, 2-year, non-paid internship at the radio station. To this day, most people in Sandusky don't know in those early days that I was the kid on the radio doing commercials because they didn't want the public to know a Negro kid, who could deliver, was the *"Voice."* Many years later, a Black man named Dudley Harris, whose on-air name was "Dudley D," would become the first Black personality WLEC would publicly acknowledge.

Athletics, coupled with conditioning and discipline, is a

Baseball Team in Sandusky, Ohio

*High School Football
Team Hall of Fame
Picture in Sandusky,
Ohio*

way to make it in life.
Take care of your mind and body and they will
Take care of you.

Sandusky, Ohio, is a city that loves its sports. If you're a star athlete, you have it made. From sixth grade to my senior year in high school, I only lost two football games. I lost once in sixth grade when we played for the citywide championship and once in high school in my senior year when we were Runner-up Statewide Champions in Ohio High School Football. My junior year, we were Ohio State High School Football Champions. Our entire football team was inducted into the High School Football Hall of Fame to commemorate our remarkable achievement.

I want to thank Coach Tony Manafo who taught me the value of teamwork, discipline and toughness during my junior high school years, Coach Eugene Kidwell for giving me the opportunity to play defense in high school, and Coach Earl Bruce, who went on to coach the Ohio State University Buckeyes, for providing me with motivation and a program from grade school to high school that instilled a Champion's heart in me.

My other sports distinctions include Little League and Babe Ruth Baseball League All Star Game MVP honors. I also lettered in football, basketball and track. These feats were accomplished through Christ, with great coaching, great teachers and my father, who was my personal trainer. They all encouraged and demanded excellence from me every step of the way!

I also credit my father with my continued interest in firearms. On occasion, he would take me hunting with him and his buddies. I can still remember the first time I fired one of his shotguns and its kickback knocked me down. They all laughed at me; however, it was a "rite of passage."

My father said, "Boy, get up and try it again!"

I did repeatedly. You see, they accepted me into their "All-Male" club. Eventually, I stopped obliterating the rabbits I shot and started bringing down game you could eat. That is, I became an accurate shot.

Lessons Learned & Thoughts to Ponder:
1. Don't be afraid of change and relocation--be willing to go where opportunities exist.

2. Remember, the Devil can and will open doors for you and tempt you too. (Matthew 4:8-11).

3. Have a passion to learn and read. Overcome obstacles and speech impediments so that you sound educated and intelligent and can communicate with <u>all</u> cultures.

4. Take advantage of internships, or create one.

5. Have a strong work ethic.

6. Always do more than you are asked to do even if

there is no compensation offered.

7. Athletics will make you mentally tough and physically fit!

8. Develop a Champion's Heart--win and never give up or quit.

9. Music—Parents and Sister's Influence. Appreciate and respect the Arts.

10. Radio is my passion that now includes multi-media. Don't be afraid to increase and expand your vision or career path.

11. If you, or a loved one, are considering a career in media, be willing to work harder than anybody else to succeed. If you are not willing to put the work in, consider a different career path. Slackers and slothful individuals need not apply!

CHAPTER THREE

Choices

"And if it seems evil to you to serve the Lord, choose for yourselves this day whom you will serve."
– Joshua 24:15

Seek God First and Don't Allow Anybody to Turn You from Him

As a youth, my first introduction to organized religion started with my grandmother, "Mama Etchin," during the summers I spent with her. She was her church's pianist, choir director, lead vocalist and chief cook. I watched her religiously read her Bible every day and have my sister, brother and I recite scripture with her. She also had her own home-based Bible Study, which meant there were always church folks in her home, along with plenty of praise and worship and delicious food, as she vigorously banged out hymn after hymn on her piano. This ignited my passion for God's Word. This also meant whenever the church was open, we were there with her.

Grandma Esther's piano

Religion was also a major part of my mother's life, too. This meant church on Sundays, sometimes Bible Study and involvement in various church programs and services. Both my grandmother and mother taught me to tithe and make offerings. I was a good church boy, obedient to the wishes of the two most important women in my life!

On the other hand, my father didn't go to church and didn't have much use for religion. His saving grace was that he didn't discourage me from going. Later in my father's life, when I was an adult and married, God used me to lead my dad to Christ! My father told me that he had watched me all my life and saw how I had really changed from my evil ways. He said, "You love and respect your wife and children and are following Christ. I want what you have, son. Please show me how?"

I recited various Romans Road scriptures with my father, and he accepted Jesus as his Lord and Savior. Praise God!

It was at about the age of 9, I first started to re-think my attitude toward religion and God. Several factors contributed to this paradigm shift in my spirituality, impacted by the actions of adults in my life who had an air of respectability, yet were flawed. First, I learned the details of my father's criminal past and present, from his cousins and close friends (some of whom were crooks themselves), my uncles, aunt and other family members. Then I reflected on my Italian mentor, who was also an undercover gangster, who led a double life. My Jewish business mentor, who regularly put his finger on the scale when weighing up items for customers that increased its cost, who cheated people and made them feel good about it, further clouded my spiritual vision. I would then learn that some Pastors at the time were prone to going in and out of backdoors, ministering to various women in the church at different times of the day, and especially evenings when their husbands worked on the second or third shifts. This practice is still prevalent today, along with pedophile priests, preying on young children, causing believers to question the sanctity of God's Church.

Finally, there was the influence of my grandmother, who, while a religious woman, was just as comfortable and had equal enthusiasm saying, "Praise the Lord," as shooting at you if you crossed her. It was too much for me to comprehend at my young age.

Me playing drums with Sam & The Crawlers Band

The Devil Will Use Glitz, Glamour and Sex to Draw You into His Web of Sin

The straw that broke the camel's back was when I learned how to play the drums and joined Sam & The Crawlers Band. This took me down a slippery slope riddled with enticing temptations in nightclubs when I was about

13 years of age. I could only perform in the nightclubs, but then would have to go into the kitchen or designated room between sets because of my age. At big shows in halls and auditoriums, I didn't have to leave the room.

However, the combination of these two circumstances led to my meeting a succession of "dirty old women" who sexually abused and exploited me. Yes, women are guilty of sexual predation and exploitation, too. Today, women of this type give young men credit or debit cards, Xboxes, video games and an assortment of other things in exchange for sexual favors and serving as their escort. Being a star athlete, I had my choice of young girls who wanted to be with me. However, these older women did and taught me things I never knew existed, literally blowing my mind! The money and explicit sex they gave me in abundance took me down a morally decadent path that would take me years to overcome.

The Devil had me in a tight-fisted grip. I was hooked on sex, booze, drugs and vanity while being a teenager. Next, I became associated with an assortment of street-level gangsters, thugs, loan sharks, prostitutes, con artists, gamblers and drug dealers who drew me deeper into their unholy lifestyle. Everybody wanted to give the drummer some because I was great at what I did and the women constantly said I was cute, turning my head in the process. I was first given the nickname of "Suggie" because women said I was so sweet. This exceeded earlier experiences when

I used to sell girls and women kisses when I was about five years old and they would actually pay me. The band experience took things to an altogether "New Level." My childhood friends and gangster associates (who are alive) still call me Suggie to this day.

Playing in the band was the period when I formally entered a life of illicit sex, criminality and turning my back on God. I also developed a split personality, too. During the day, I was a normal, mannerly and innocent looking student-athlete who achieved good grades and excelled in sports. I completed my homework assignments during study halls or immediately after school was out.

But at night, unbeknownst to most of my peers, I was a scheming criminal who hired adults to serve as my minions. I also enjoyed a succession of old and young women, who were willing to enthusiastically do my sexual biddings. Unfortunately, there was no **#METOO Movement** for young men available to protect me from sexual exploitation and predation by females. At first, I couldn't believe the adults and women would do my biddings. I was too young to drive a car so they drove me around. I opened several gambling joints (through surrogates) that led to bootlegging, prostitution, fencing activity, loan sharking, strong arm enforcement and drug dealing.

Later in life, I had removed the thought of my running these gambling joints from my mind, however, during a visit to home, my youngest brother, Kenny, reminded me of what I had done and drove me around to the areas. Old memories returned. In terms of gambling, I was poor with cards but especially good at shooting craps (dice). I could hold, shake and switch two pairs of dice in one hand without a person knowing it. Of course, one set of dice was crooked and the other good. This meant I could win or lose whenever I chose. I mostly chose to win so I cheated people out of their hard-earned money. I had suckers lined up bringing their payroll cash to me, attempting to get even from losing the previous week. My big "flash" roll of money kept the suckers lined up for a shot at me.

I practiced equal opportunity and beat all comers, regardless of their ethnicity or age because I didn't care. It also helped that I had two of my associates, who were known to carry pistols and knives always with me, just in case one of my suckers physically attempted to take their money back. I'd start a crap game with one or two suckers, then took turns allowing myself, or one of my associates to win. We'd let the sucker win just enough to keep him engaged in the game until we eventually picked him clean. This opened the door to loan sharking since many of them didn't want to go home broke and face the wrath of their wife, or woman. Of course, I charged the going loan shark rate.

As good as I was with the dice, every now and then I screwed up and got caught cheating. My associates and I would have to pull out our pistols to get out of the room or hallway in one piece. This happened in two predominately white bars. One of my associates (the wheel man) would run and start the car and the other and I would shoot up the door so they couldn't get to us. The wheel man would then shoot up the door, after we escaped to pin our victims down until we got in the car.

This got too nerve-wracking for me so I turned to pad rolling dice. That is rolling dice on a blanket. I would blow on the dice in my hand, but was really spitting on the dice thus locking them up on combinations of 7 or 11 or on craps, depending on how I wanted the dice to fall. This minimized being caught with crooked dice but still allowed me to cheat based on what combinations I wanted to fall and when. There's a saying in business, "If it sounds too good to be true, it usually is!" Remember; things are not necessarily as they appear to be, and greed can get you killed.

I was truly connected during this season, selling liquor while I didn't drink and hard drugs while I was not a user, except for smoking some potent weed from time to time. I learned early on to never be your own best customer. I lived various forms of this double life from middle school to my early 20s. I had dropped my sinful ways at the age of 24 when I would meet the woman who would become my wife and help me end my life of crime and return to God.

Gwen and me in formal attire

*Good Intentions not Rooted in Christ
Don't Often Come to Fruition*

After graduating from high school, I left Sandusky to go to college with a goal of becoming a full-time student and a part-time criminal. Instead, I became a full-time criminal and a part-time student. I was still an avid reader of books. This time my nightstand was filled with "How to Pimp-type books" such as *Pimp*, and *Trick Baby* that were written and actually lived out by the legendary Pimp and Con Artist, Iceberg Slim. I also enjoyed Eldridge Cleaver's *Soul on Ice* and Malcolm X's *The Autobiography of Malcolm X*.

Pimp and *Trick Baby* gave me insight into hustling at a higher level and perfecting my life as a "Con Artist." *Soul on Ice* and Malcolm X's *The Autobiography of Malcolm X* drew me toward my own Blackness and the struggle of black people to overcome oppression. However, despite reading about the struggle, I still enjoyed being a gangster with all the perks that came with the role. Since I was now away from Sandusky, Ohio, I expanded my operation and my illicit trade exploded! However, the lack of God's presence in my life would gnaw at my soul, often leaving me with emptiness and no joy in my material abundance and relationships. I could feel the Devil's presence who was guiding the work of my hands. I would experience what I thought were successes, but they were hollow.

Despite this realization, I organized my various lines of criminal activities and ran them like a business, while keeping an extremely low profile, as my organized Italian crime mentor instructed me to do (*Incognito Gangster*). He operated in the mode of old-style gangsters who shunned publicity and notoriety. So, I set many people up as fronts who gladly served me as they became wealthy. I learned early in the game that the world is full of people willing and ready to sell anybody out at the drop of a hat. And there is no short supply of these types of individuals, who exist both in and outside of the church. Those who worked for me all understood the dire consequences of stealing from me, or turning snitch. None of them wanted a visit from the enforcement side of my business. One demonstration was all they needed. That's all I'll say about this.

You Gradually Descend into Having a Reprobate Mind.
It Doesn't Happen Overnight.

Of all my criminal activities, I enjoyed being a grifter and con artist the most. Playing the "Short and Long" con was exhilarating. It takes a special and patient person to be a successful con artist. It's a person, who has ice water flowing through their veins, and the capability of lying to you with a straight face, while making you believe they're sincere. A good con artist plays on a person's greed and makes them believe they're getting over on him, while the focus of the con called a "Pidgeon or Mark," is the one really being taken to the cleaners getting ripped off from his/her money and sometimes soul, too.

The master teachings of pimp and con artist, Iceberg Slim and his books, *Pimp* and *Trick Baby*, guided me to becoming a more slick, cunning and ruthless predator. Deception is one of the key tactics of the Devil who is the ultimate Deceiver. And I was enthusiastically walking with Satan during this period of my life and was easily devouring all whom I met. I could not believe how gullible most people were.

This fact was true then and still so today. There's credence in the saying, "A sucker is born every 60 seconds!" I thank God for keeping my "Old Man" in check today.

During my criminal life after high school, I would wake up each day, shower and dress just like most normal people. Next, I would proceed to put on my shoulder holster and gun, strap on my secondary ankle holster and gun, and conceal an assortment of knives and other weapons on my person to be readily accessible, if needed. Then, I would have meetings with my various lieutenants about planned activities and proceeds. To those of you who personally know me, you will find this hard to accept and believe that I was such a ruthless, vicious man, but yes, this was true. You see, I was good at being an *Incognito Gangster*.

God's Grace Causes it to Rain on the Just and the Unjust.
He will Keep You Despite Yourself.

Allow me to digress for a moment from adulthood to adolescence and draw some parallels from my youth that guided me as an adult. During my years as a teenager marked the first time I was shot at, which taught me to always protect myself at all times. I never will forget the time when Sam Dickerson, our band leader, and I got into an argument with a bar owner who stiffed us on his payment to us for playing at his bar. I was standing between Sam and the bar owner, who in the heat of the argument, pulled out his pistol, shot at me but hit Sam.

Folks, this all took place some 44 years ago. I'm reminded though of a popular Sci-Fi movie trilogy, wherein the main character reaches the point in his life when his powers enhance and everything slows down during confrontations. You know the scene when he can see slow, revolving bullets coming at him, as he dodged them, while they appeared to be moving in slow motion and unable to hit him as they whizzed past. This was the same experience I had. Nothing could touch me.

Little did I know that God's angels were protecting me from being killed during this incident and countless other times, when thugs and other gangsters were trying to take me out because I bested them at the "Game."

Another example of God's grace occurred when I was about 17 years old. A group of my friends and I had been up all night roller skating, partying and were traveling back to Sandusky at about 3 a.m. I was driving and fell asleep at the wheel during a snowy winter night. I lost control of the car and slid down a steep, icy embankment in Vermilion, Ohio, crashing into a tree. It was pitch black and you couldn't see your hands or feet in front of you. Thank God, no one was injured. We got out of the car and I instinctively started walking back up the incline. The next morning, I came back with my father and a tow truck to retrieve my car. I saw that my car's fall had been stopped by a big tree. I was shocked to see that a mere two feet beyond that tree was over a couple of hundred feet straight drop into a frozen Lake Erie. If not for that tree, we all would have plunged into the icy, deep frigid waters below and possibly died. Plus, if I had walked forward I would have fallen over the cliff and probably would have died, too. Not only did God save me, but all my passengers, too. One of those passengers, who was a close criminal associate of mine, went on to become a Deacon in his church today! God, bless you, Deacon David (Huntsy) Jones.

As I stated at the beginning of this book, it is not meant to be a ***How-to Book on Crime*** that glorifies criminal activity. Rather, this book will help its reader recognize and draw on both the positive and negative life experiences in their personal quest to find themselves in Christ.

Lessons Learned and Thoughts to Ponder:

1. Introduction to Christianity and Crime—a person can live a Double Life.

2. Christianity—meeting and knowing God is a life-long process, filled with twists and turns.

3. Crime—is evil and always present—revealing itself in numerous incognito manifestations.

   a. Organized Crime Connections

   b. Drug Dealer

   c. After-Hour Joints

   d. Loan Sharking

   e. Gambling

   f. Strong Arming

   g. Playboys—Playgirls

   h. Pimping

   i. Grifter and Con Artist

   j. Complete Gangster

4. Sexual abuse of any child can happen and is wrong. Sexual abuse of boys by women is real and does happen. Don't just be on the lookout for sexual abuse of girls by men. Guard all your children from all potential sexual predators (Secular and in the Church).

5. Choices—God gives us free will to accept or reject His ways. Always make informed decisions. I made a personal decision to begin thinking about getting out of the Game.

   a. Never be pressured into making a quick decision.

   b. Pressure to take advantage of so-called good sounding deals is a trick of the Devil.

6. In addition to attending a Sunday service, regularly go to Bible Study where your Pastor has time to focus on teachings that will build up your spiritual maturity and discernment of good versus evil. (*Hebrews 5:12-14*). This will also aid you in resisting a multitude of demons, con artists, bad deals and those seeking to separate you from your money. My pastor, Pastor John K. Jenkins Sr., has a teaching called "Discerning God's Voice—5 Ways." These power-packed messages address many of the critical financial decisions we make that have long-lasting impacts.

7. You don't have to physically be in a church to let God use you to lead a person to Christ. Know how to minister to people and lead them through Romans Road scriptures to salvation. Read Romans Chapter 10 Verses 9 & 10.

CHAPTER FOUR

Broadcasting-Media Relations Career

"For we do not wrestle against flesh and blood, but against principalities, against powers, against rulers of the darkness of this age, against the spiritual hosts of wickedness in heavenly places."
– Ephesians 6:12

Sometimes you can make the right decision,
Despite it being for the wrong motive.

My entry into broadcasting was the beginning of stopping my street-level criminal behavior, activities and associations. I did this for practical reasons and not for any great religious epiphany. I still had plenty of women who did things for me. But half way through my broadcast career and spiritual maturity growth, the scriptural significance of **Ephesians 6:10—20** took on new meaning. The operative verse to me is *Ephesians 6:12*. I knew that Satan is the "Prince of the Air." I also knew that broadcasting is transmitted via RF frequencies, microwave and satellites.

As I was studying this scripture one day, the correlation between Satan and the airwaves I used to transmit my broadcasts leapt off the pages of the Bible. I realized that my chosen profession was a medium controlled and used by Satan to advance his agenda. It was then that I knew I had to daily put on the whole armor of God to survive.

In my later years, when I was in All-Time ministry, I conveyed this truism to my Audio Visual (AV) Staff and ministry associates about the nature of the medium we're in. Some heard and stayed prayed up, but some didn't. On Sundays, Satan, or one of his minions, doesn't always go straight to the pulpit or Music Ministry when he comes to church.

I know that he also goes to the AV Department, where he can interfere with both reception of the preached word and Music Ministry by causing unnecessary feedback and transmission issues, due to sloppiness by operators and those who are not prayed up before they serve. These unnecessary distractions impede countless numbers of people from hearing, or seeing, God's Words, thus impeding spiritual growth.

Out of Darkness the Light was Turned On

Always seek knowledge and wisdom.
Success is the product of hard work and diligence.

When I left Sandusky after high school to attend college at The Ohio State University in Columbus, Ohio, I thought I was ready to compete for a job in radio and television. Wrong. I had a new hunting ground ripe with all ethnicities of women that I fully enjoyed exploiting and my life really got busy. School was secondary in my mind, at the time, and was just a means toward an end. It was coming too slow for me while in school.

So, after several years, I dropped out to attend and graduate from the WIXY School of Broadcasting in Cleveland, Ohio, held at the number one radio station in the market at the time. WIXY had a comprehensive, concentrated curriculum that focused on programming, vocal delivery, writing and production skills that included editing and complex over-dubs taught by its on-air announcers who were at the top of their profession.

WIXY-AM/FM was a combo operation. FM had an Easy Listening format and its AM was a traditional Top 40 formatted radio station. WIXY-AM/FM was an ABC Radio affiliate and frequently served as a host site that legendary broadcaster and commentator, Paul Harvey, often used when in Cleveland to uplink his daily broadcast. I rubbed shoulders with Paul Harvey and watched how he would rip wire copy, the very same wire copy I ripped, that he would use in his broadcast commentaries. He would go to a typewriter and bang out his copy that he would then read over the air. It was the same thing I was doing, only much better and punctuated with his folksy delivery. His influence led me to finding my broadcast style as it related to the delivery of news.

WIXY Newsman Mel Luck, who went by the on-air name of Alexander Prescott, taught me how to do a stentorian, up-tempo Top 40 News delivery that eloquently punctuated key words as well as a traditional, authoritative News delivery for use on FM, Easy Listening, or All News formatted radio stations. Billy Bass, who came up in R&B formats in Cleveland, crossed over to WIXY-AM. He really taught me how to make it into mainstream radio and influenced me how to also make it in TV.

During the evenings and weekends in Cleveland, I hung out at R&B stations WABQ-AM and WJMO-AM. Lynn (Shotgun) Tolliver, Mike Payne and Chuck Denson were some of my mentors. This, in addition to my growing up in Sandusky, listening to these guys from long distance, helped. Top Jock Tom Shannon and the Newscasters on the high powered 50,000 watt CKLW-AM radio station out of Windsor, Canada, situated just across the river from Detroit, Michigan, blazed a trail across Middle America influencing other broadcasters. CKLW's pumping Top 40 Music complete with dramatic station drop-overs, laced with tympani and blaring brass, coupled with a fast-paced News format shaped and molded me, too. I was enthralled and in broadcast heaven!

I was so totally immersed in broadcasting, at this point in my life, that I put my life of crime on hold, along with most of my women. To date, I had evaded being arrested for criminal activities. I wanted to fully get out of the game badly because I knew any arrest would potentially give me negative press and be detrimental to my long-term career interests. So, I became a complete student and trainee. Remember, I was still an avid reader.

One day as I was visiting a bookstore on the campus of Case Western Reserve University in Cleveland, Ohio, I stumbled across a book entitled, *Yes I Can: The Story of Sammy Davis Jr.* I read it cover-to-cover in one day on the same day I purchased it. I've since read it numerous other times, too. Next to the Holy Bible, this book has had the most profound impact on my life and self-awareness. *Yes I Can* is a self-portrait of one of the most extraordinary men of our time, who became a figure of controversy because he dared to live his life not as a Negro, but as a man.

For a point of reference, during this period in time Black people stopped being referred to as Colored, but as Negroes. Sammy was billed as "the greatest living entertainer in the world" because he was a singer, dancer, actor and comedian who broke color barriers in his day in the recording industry, major entertainment venues, Las Vegas, films and television. Sammy Davis Jr. was born in the same year my mother was born so they experienced similar types of discrimination. I could relate to his life and attitude he had toward overcoming discrimination without being outwardly bitter.

Toxicity will drive people away from you, regardless of color, or the validity of how wronged you have been done.

WSOK-AM Radio in
Savannah, Georgia—My first full-time Radio Job

Several weeks after graduating from the WIXY School of Broadcasting, I received a fulltime job offer to be an on-air announcer (DJ) at WSOK-AM Radio in Savannah, Georgia. I'll never forget the look on my father's face as he drove me in his shiny Cadillac to the Cleveland Hopkins International Airport for my flight to Savannah. He was proud and happy for me; however, he had an air of bewilderment about himself. Based on everything I had done in my life, both good and bad, plus overcoming being a chronic stutterer, here I was off to a job of being a radio announcer, talking to large numbers of people for a living. Despite my academic and athletic successes, this was the first time I had shared a special moment of this type with my father and we both really felt good about it. In retrospect, I was also bewildered and amazed at the time of my accomplishment, too.

I was picked up at Savannah's airport by the announcer whose position I was taking. I didn't know it at the time, but learned shortly after he picked me up, what the deal was. Folks, sometimes the Radio & TV business is cold and unfeeling. After I settled in, I met the man who hired me. Jimmy "The Gator" Lang, who not only was WSOK's Program Director, but was a broadcasting legend, too. He immediately cut me into the fabric of Savannah's community. One such relationship was with a man called Willie Brown. Willie was Black and was a reporter for one of the local Savannah TV stations.

Occasionally, Willie and I would hang out with each other. One night he drew an assignment to cover a Ku Klux Klan cross burning. Willie invited me to go on assignment with him. I said to myself this guy who is Black, is either crazy or incredibly brave, and he's going to cover a cross burning and didn't seem worried about it.

So, I tagged along just to see what would happen. I instinctively reached for my pistol and frantically realized that since I had gone straight, I didn't have my trusty old piece with me anymore. I felt naked and under-dressed for the occasion. Willie and I drove out into the pitch-black countryside that was devoid of any street lights. Suddenly, out of nowhere we could see a blazing fire emanating from the burning cross that lit up the darkness and night sky.

We got out of his car despite my apparent reluctance. Next, Willie said to the Klan members, "How are you boys doing tonight?" As they started talking, he began calling some of them by their first names, despite them having their faces covered. I concluded that Willie knew them since before his television career he was a fireman and probably had to make runs to their frequent cross burnings. Meanwhile, they exchanged pleasantries, gave Willie the shots and were very helpful and meticulous in giving him the background and their message of hate he needed for his story. Then everybody pleasantly said good night. I was dumbfounded!

Willie and I got back into his car and drove away. I was still a bit shaken and in disbelief about what had just transpired. I asked him to step on the gas and get out of there before those "Good Ole Boys" changed their attitudes and minds!

Jimmy "The Gator" Lang also taught me about commercial production, on-air delivery, and pacing and event promotion. I watched him closely and learned how to be both a personality and a promoter. Jimmy had a promotion and production company called "Jam Alligator Productions." He and a team of gorgeous women, known as the "Gatorettes," uniquely promoted his concerts on radio and at the street level by putting up posters and hyping his events in clubs, barber shops, beauty salons and everywhere people were gathered. They were also present the day of the event, handling ticket sales and getting people to their seats.

This was the first time I had seen such a smooth, efficient operation as this. I vividly remember when "The Gator" first introduced me to James Brown, "The Godfather of Soul." I had the opportunity, on many occasions, to fly on James Brown's personal jet and got front row tickets to his concerts. My relationship with James Brown lasted for the rest of his life, regardless of what city I was in, or station I worked for; I was always graciously welcomed by the "Godfather" because of Jimmy "The Gator" Lang.

Many people outside of the entertainment business did not know until the movie, *Get On Up*, was released that James Brown used Black promoters to promote his concerts across the country, keeping money in our community. Jimmy Lang was one of James Brown's promoters so I learned from the best.

Little would I know that years later at my home church, the First Baptist Church of Glenarden in suburban Washington, DC, that I would run into Jay Lang, Jimmy Lang's son, who is also an announcer and broadcaster. Jay remains a good friend of mine. Jay Lang is in ministry with me and is a business associate that I regularly use as the voiceover talent on various video and radio projects, in addition to being the chief voice of my radio network called the ***Praise Power Network***. Personal relationships are everything in the world of media and business.

PraisePowerNetwork.com is the Internet address to log on and listen 24/7 to some of the best gospel and inspirational music in the world.

In the Right Place at the Right Time.

"The Lord, before whom I walk, will send His
angel with you and prosper your way ..."
– Genesis 24:40

After working several years at WSOK Radio, I was ready to return to Columbus, Ohio, and resume my education and work in a larger radio and television market. Discrimination was rampant in the broadcasting industry, during the 1960s and 1970s. Radio and television stations, through lawsuits before the FCC challenging their licenses, were put under intense pressure to hire minorities, if they wanted to keep those precious licenses. Newspapers felt the pressure, too. This was also the time that many Black broadcasters saw job opportunities now open to them that never existed before.

I discovered that all the major commercial radio and TV stations in Columbus, Ohio, funded and cooperated from a training perspective an effort called *The Skills Bank Program* administered by The Ohio State University. The program provided course work at Ohio State University and a choice of radio and television stations from which to learn in addition to classes at the university. I applied and was accepted. I choose Taft Broadcasting which had an AM/FM radio combo operation and TV station Channel 6. I also, received training at WBNS-TV too. I was a newscaster on Taft's AM station and newscaster and DJ on its FM station. On Channel 6, I received training as a TV Director and learned television production that included producing commercials and long & short form programs. I did the same type of television production at WBNS-TV. I was also taught how to write, dress properly and announce at a level I had never imagined conforming to mainstream media requirements.

After completing the two-year program, Taft Broadcasting hired me as an announcer for its FM station and had me do directing work on its TV station too. Pete "The Angel" Gabriel, Taft's FM Program Director, was instrumental in my rise in the company. Taft's radio outlets were situated on the top floor of one the highest buildings in Columbus and had a panoramic view of the city. I invited my Father to come down from Sandusky and visit me while I was on the air one night. When he stepped off the elevator into the station lobby he saw the panoramic view of the city and bright lights and was awestricken only saying, "WOW!"

It all came together and he was amazed at what God had allowed me to achieve. I told him, "Dad, my next stop is Washington, DC, for bigger and better things!" However, that night we both enjoyed the moment and took in the tremendous view from the top!

Columbus, Ohio, represented a tremendous period of growth and development for me. I formed relationships with legendary broadcasters such as Eddie Saunders, Bill Moss, Chuck White, Les Brown "The Motivator," Bob Gooding and entertainers such as Duke Ellington, Lou Rawls, Young-Holt Unlimited Trio, Nancy Wilson, Rusty Bryant, actor and singer John Davidson, Billy Davis and The Fifth Dimension just to name a few.

Several true stories: Duke Ellington was appearing at one of the local nightclubs and I was given the assignment to go out and get a personal interview with the "Duke." When I arrived at the club, most of the Columbus area Radio and TV media was there for the same purpose. I thought to myself, *how can I pull this off with all the big-name reporters there for the same reason?*

After his show was over, we were all lined up outside of the Duke's dressing room door, waiting to interview him. He came out, surveyed who was there and said to me, "Young man, you're first."

I went forward with much fear and trembling into his dressing room. I told him that I had never interviewed a legend of his stature such as him before and that he was my first. Mr. Ellington was patient and gracious with me. He told me that his firsts were always at the highest level in his career be it major clubs, films or television. He told me that there was something special about me that drew him to me and that the other reporters could wait until he and I were finished.

My interview with Duke Ellington instilled in me the desire to always deal at the top and not be afraid of doing great things! Shortly after the Ellington interview, I drew the assignment to go and get an interview with Nancy Wilson, who was appearing at a major department store to introduce her new line of cosmetic products. I figured

I was on a roll since I was the only black face in a sea of white reporters.

Nancy Wilson was fine and shapely! She singled me out for an interview. After the interview was over, I told her that she was beautiful, I was in love with her and that I wanted to take her out on a date. She told me she was flattered, but I was too young for her. She did give me a big kiss, and I almost fainted on the floor of the Lazarus Department store. Everybody had a big laugh at my expense; however, I got to kiss Nancy Wilson on her lips and not on her cheek! I remembered that Duke Ellington told me to always deal at the top! Nancy Wilson was the top and she was a classy lady, too.

Sometimes you must move yourself and
have a Wilderness Experience.

I could have remained in Columbus, Ohio, and been a big fish in a medium-size market and lived, well—happily ever after. However, I wanted more and desired to function as a newsman at a national level in a major market. The National Black News Network, or NBN, was based in New York City, New York, and the Mutual Black News Network, or MBN, was based in Washington, DC. Since Washington, DC is the political and news capitol of the country, it was my logical choice.

Plus, I knew Chuck Denson, who was a newsman on Mutual, from my days in Cleveland. Chuck had been telling me for years that he had a three-hour on-air shift every day and one hour of production for a total work day of only four hours, five days a week and was making insane money in the process. His biggest worry was getting a tee time each day, or which lady he would play tennis with and entertain. Chuck was living the good life in a city that had a severe shortage of men too! The ratio of women to men I was told was about six to one. Great numbers for a single man who loved having plenty of women!

At the time, I left Columbus, I was in strong contention for a news anchor job at the Mutual Black Network, but it never happened. I found myself in the Nation's Capital with no job, no immediate prospects and my money was running low since I was no longer a gangster. I was faced with either going back to Columbus, Ohio, in defeat, which was not an option, turning back to crime, which was out, or taking a dead-end job. I resisted going back to my criminal activities and, for about two weeks, I was homeless in Washington, DC in the summer time so it wasn't too bad.

Yes, Tom Pope slept on park benches because I didn't want to go to a shelter. I was too proud to ask anybody for help, but did cry out to God who heard my plea. He put several things in my path. I called my family and tried to make out that I was doing well. My grandmother and mother sensed I was not doing well and sent me some money via Western Union to get a room, feed myself and have funds to look for a job. After moving from a succession of rooms that also included meals, I settled in at McLean Gardens in upper Northwest DC.

There, I met a person who would become my life-long friend (BFF) and Godfather to my children, Gerald Draper. Next, I got a job at Georgetown Texaco pumping gas. My how great the mighty had fallen! God allowed me to be stripped of my arrogance, pride, (which goeth before the fall) working a minimum wage job before He could use me. Please don't get judgmental when I reveal what happened to me next. I did have a relapse of sin around gambling and started a recurring crap game in the back room of the gas station in the heart of Georgetown. I easily started winning more money than I earned pumping gas. Suckers making the bus transfer would stop in between bus transfers and end up giving me their money going home broke. There was an endless supply of suckers.

I soon moved into the fashionable Black peoples' address at the time in Southeast DC to a high-rise building with panoramic views of the city called the Marbury Plaza apartments. I also bought myself a red convertible VW car that was low profile. My days of being broke and penniless in DC were over and finally in the rearview mirror!

A notorious bank robber back in the "Roaring 20s" was often asked why he robbed banks. His response was simple, "Because that's where the money is!"

Washington, DC was the mecca for Black radio so that's where I went to seek my fame and fortune and eventually meet my wife.

I was blessed to have landed in Washington, DC in the early 1970s when WOL-AM and WHUR-FM radio stations were coming into their periods of greatness. Bob "The Nighthawk" Terry, whose family was from Kentucky, was the premier announcer and Program Director at WHUR-FM. I sent Bob an unsolicited audition tape and was blown off by him.

So, I called his family in Kentucky and told them who I was, where I was from in Kentucky, how good of an announcer I was, and how Bob had treated me. The next day Bob called me and we had a spirited discussion that he laced with plenty of expletives. Nighthawk also told me that I didn't have to tell on him and that I had a job at WHUR-FM. He closed by calling me a few more choice expletives and welcomed me aboard the staff in what would be my first tour of duty at WHUR-FM Radio.

The format at WHUR-FM during this period focused on the whole spectrum of black music called "360 Degrees of Blackness." On-air announcers were referred to as Producers back then. Some played radical message music;

others played R&B, Jazz, Caribbean or Gospel music. In an area designated as *The People's Platform* in a building called "Tempo-C," news and talk programming originated. Frequent guests to the People's Platform included H. Rap Brown, Stokely Carmichael (Kwame Ture), who coined the phrase "Black Power," and a host of global, national and local political activists.

It was rough and tumble at WHUR during that era. Sometimes I felt I was in one of my old gangster meetings in terms of weaponry. If I start naming names of broadcast legends I worked beside and formed life-long relationships with at WHUR-FM, I'll get into trouble so I'm not going to do it because most of them came to the meetings "packing" something themselves. I do encourage you to visit the station and view its Hall of Fame of Broadcasters list where you can observe the names of those persons I know and knew.

My first tour of duty at WHUR-FM also laid the groundwork for my better understanding of African History and contributions Black people made to civilization from the beginning of time. I also met top artists, politicians and celebrities, with whom I've maintained relationships with today.

After a season, God moved on my heart and told me it was time to leave WHUR-FM and broaden my horizons in the area of governmental broadcasting. This also marked my entry into a freelance era of broadcasting. I landed a job as a writer for the Voice of America English News Division whose name has since changed. I started on the Africa and Asian Desks, then worked the Middle East Desk, finally settling on the U.S. Desk. Because English is the second language for most listeners of the Voice of America broadcasts, my writing had to be crisp, succinct and devoid of any type of political assessments. And of course, my scripts had to be pro-United States.

This was challenging for me, based on my Afro-centric indoctrination at WHUR-FM. So, I went through a period of intense editing from my superiors until I got with the program. I also did many freelance radio programs as both talent and producer, did some short film voiceovers and acted in several U.S. Department of Housing and Urban Development (HUD) films, the most notable being, *Be It Ever So Humble*.

This was an exceptional period of professional growth for me. It also enhanced my entrepreneurial spirit and grew my confidence in not having a regular job and paycheck, meaning I had to hustle if I wanted to pay the bills, which I did and **NOT** have a relapse as an *Incognito Gangster*. Plus, I had growing confidence in God that He would open doors of opportunity for me.

After my first tour of duty at WHUR-FM, the Voice of America experience and freelance career, I went to work for WYCB-AM, a Gospel formatted radio station located in the National Press Building in downtown Washington,

DC. Its motto was *"A Station With a Heart in the Heart of the City."* WYCB's AM signal literally blanketed DC, which was known as *"Chocolate City"* at the time because of its huge Black population. Its Program Director and afternoon drive personality, who hired me, was Vashti McKenzie, who would go onto to become Bishop Vashti McKenzie, a Bishop in the African Methodist Episcopal (AME) Church. I'm so proud of Vashti's spiritual growth and development and various organizations she has created and books she has written to help people.

Other key personalities included Lou *The Morning Spirit* Hankins, Jaqueline Gales, Dr. Lucille Banks Robinson Miller, Dr. Calvin W. Rolark, Ralph Petey Greene, Harold Bell and yours truly Tom Pope. With this tremendous lineup of personalities, WYCB was a perennial Top 5 and #1 radio station in the market. These giants in the business also made me a significant part of Black DC as well as the rest of the city. I learned so much from them, including mixing gospel music, showmanship, promotion and secured strong political contacts that would aid me later in my media relations career.

Petey Greene also made me a production assistant on his weekly TV show. On air, he used to call me the "Linebacker-Looking Nigger." At first, I thought Petey was popular only in the Black community, which he was. Later, I discovered that whites along with other ethnic groups knew and loved him, too. He was the type of person that if you walked down the street with him, you'd be stopped every few feet with people who either acknowledged him, wanted to talk or holler out his name on the street, or shout from passing cars and taxicabs. One other person and friend I knew who was this way was the late Dr. Betty Shabazz, Malcom X's widow. More on Dr. Betty later in my book.

Suffering from radio-fatigue, I took a break from broadcasting and took a job in the airline industry to broaden my view of the world. This move allowed me to visit every continent, most world capitals and further develop my world view. It was on Ipanema Beach in Rio de Janeiro, South America, that I really met my future wife who was from Northeast, Washington, DC so I made the first move and started our romance. I had seen her in DC and had limited interaction. Up until then, I didn't have her phone number. Finally I got her digits!

On the long, overnight flight back to the states, I continued romancing her and asked her to end the relationship she was in and start seeing me exclusively. Instead, she put me on hold! I wasn't used to a woman turning me down.

Gwen was slender and had big beautiful, penetrating eyes. So, I thought to myself she would probably fill out later in life but still look attractive. Prior to our meeting each other, she had and was traveling the world alone, which takes a lot of courage, plus she was a sophisticated woman. Gwen was naive to my world of gangsters, hustlers and thugs and that was fine with me. To me she represented everything I wanted to leave behind and keep buried in my past. I wanted to protect her with all of my life and very being because I loved her then, as I do now!

She said, "Yes, I'll marry you!" To use a popular contemporary phrase, she also said, "Yes, to the Dress!"

She looked so beautiful in her wedding gown. When I think of that image of her on our wedding day, it is an image forever etched in my mind.

Gwen & Tom Pope on their wedding day

WHUR-FM second tour—being in the right place at the right time! The story of how WHUR-FM News and Information evolved into a market leader.

My second tour of duty at WHUR-FM was truly remarkable. Once again, God had put me in the right place at the right time. I could draw on all the life and broadcast experiences, as well as strong contacts I had garnered previously and apply them at Howard University's WHUR-FM. The radio station was still located in the building called Tempo-C by the reservoir. However, Howard University had decided to move the station into the building that was called Freedman's Hospital. Both the building and WHUR's format would receive extensive renovation. I never will forget the meeting I had with then WHUR General Manager, Robert *"The Black* Taylor" and Dr. Owen D. Nichols, Vice President for Administration and head of Communications at the University. Both men had brilliant minds, were innovative and extremely disciplined. Robert was a student of Machiavellian thought and Keynesian economic philosophy. This economic philosophy or theory advances that capitalism is a good economic system. And in a capitalistic system, people earn money from their work.

Businesses employ and pay people to work. Then people can spend their money on things they want.

Since we were both followers of Machiavellian thought and capitalists too, we often had long, deep philosophical discussions. WHUR-FM was doing well in Washington's radio market, however, under the leadership of Dr. James E. Cheek, Dr. Nichols and Robert Taylor, the vision for the station was expanded.

I was first hired to be a Producer, then promoted to Assistant News Director, then promoted to serve as News Director with a formal title of Director of News and Information. The News and Information aspect of programming would become more centrist moving from its current far-left editorial perspective. However, WHUR would not retreat from its commitment to news and information relevant to Black people. Rather, we would expand the comprehension of what we did. I was given the resources and latitude I needed to do the job. We got rid of our typewriters and installed an electronic newsroom complete with computer terminals. We had Associated Press (AP), United Press International (UPI), Reuters and Agency France-Presse news wires installed into our electronic news system.

I worked on the on-air delivery styles of each reporter and strengthened them in the areas where they had weakness. This was extremely difficult to accomplish, but we incorporated change for those open to change and encouraged those who couldn't get with the program to secure employment elsewhere. I then restructured the News Department creating three editors over the respective Local Desk, covering DC and local counties; Capitol Hill Desk covering both Houses of Congress and national issues; and the International Desk covering the world in general with a focus on Africa, the so-called Middle East and the Caribbean complemented with a team of free-lance reporters called stringers who filed daily reports from the various regions. The element to making this news operation excel was to appoint a Chief Editor and writer of our news that would give me consistency in our writing style and reporting content. This new division of duties and responsibilities worked extremely well and allowed the journalists to focus on their strengths knowing they had support in the News Department.

We then asked Howard's School of Communications to send us their brightest and best students to serve in our newsroom which they did. Plus, I beefed up our Sports Desk and coverage and created a team of technical producers who technically edited sound actualities for the reports as well as take in the free-lance stringers' stories. I had mentioned earlier the brilliance of Dr. Nichols and Robert Taylor. The three of us negotiated a deal with the CBS Radio Network through one of its subsidiary radio networks called CBS Radio-Radio Network. In addition to WHUR clearing (airing) some its commercial spots over our airwaves, CBS would give us a cash payment for doing so, plus provide us access to it short newscasts if we chose to air them, but more importantly, sound actualities (news bites) and network reporters' stories we could incorporate into our news if we chose.

The last key element of this deal was that CBS Radio-Radio Network would give WHUR free satellite time to uplink and downlink our remote broadcasts from major events such as the Democratic or Republican National Conventions. In 1984, we conducted our first, via satellite, coverage of those conventions to our listenership here in the metro Washington, DC area. These major enhancements gave us a global reach and our ratings during our information segments shot through the roof! We even received inquiries from the local All-News radio station about how we were doing what we were doing and beating them so badly in the Arbitron ratings. Ever since those days WHUR-FM has been a perineal Top 5 or #1 radio station in the DC market. My crowning achievements were recognition from the CBS Radio Network as its "Affiliate Editor of the Year" and "Journalist of the Year" from the Congressional Black Caucus. I could not have received this acclaim without the support of a dedicated, hard-working staff who was the best at what they did.

During the 1980s in Washington, DC, Black media (radio, TV and print) would occasionally meet to talk about mutual issues of concern. Black weekly newspapers usually went to print on Wednesdays or Thursdays and had trouble competing with the major daily newspapers, especially in terms of breaking major local stories.

For instance, DC's Mayor Marion S. Barry would have his weekly reporter's briefings early in the week around major city initiatives or issues. After explaining to him the issues the weekly Black newspapers were having in terms of breaking stories, he moved those gatherings to Wednesdays to accommodate us. This new-found sensitivity quickly spread throughout metro Washington, today called the DMV, impacting local counties and Capitol Hill, as well as resonating with the Congressional Black Caucus and other national organizations based in the Nation's Capital concerning news distribution.

Having your stories left out of the Daily Drum Newscast was devastating to those who could not get with the program, thus relegating them to irrelevance in the news cycle. Don't get judgmental. This is how the news game is played and works. Lack of access and cooperation can negatively impact a news origination's editorial perspective of you.

I have so many fond memories of my second tour of duty at WHUR-FM. The growth of WHUR's news and informational programming was phenomenal. The station already had a tight music format whose premier program was, and still is, called *The Quiet Storm*, originally hosted by the legendary Melvin Lindsey. A brief timeout for a sidebar please.

Melvin Lindsey

Melvin Lindsey transitioned; however, while he was a national mega star in broadcasting, he was better at being a good person. Despite Melvin's huge popularity, he was a down-to-earth person with a great attitude! He and I worked the same shift at WHUR and interacted daily around special programming and news in his programming segment. I never heard Melvin say one curse word or speak ill of anyone. I remember one Christmas party the station gave for the staff.

One of the main categories was, "If you were in a dark alley who would you want at your back?"

Before we filled out our ballots, Melvin Lindsey stood up and said, "That's an easy question. We all know its Tom Pope." Folks, I won the prize!

Since I worked an afternoon shift, my wife and I would go to cheap, early afternoon movie matinees, and who would we regularly see in the theatre at the Watergate complex we attended? It was Melvin Lindsey!

"Melvin," I said, "what are you doing here?" and he would say, "The same thing you're doing, Tom and Gwen—enjoying a cheap flick!"

Other WHUR-FM accomplishments.

From the 1970s through the early 1980s, WHUR would conduct a remote broadcast on the steps of Congress on Dr. Martin Luther King Jr.'s January birthday, protesting and calling for a national holiday day honoring Dr. King. Meantime, Stevie Wonder, other national artists, members of the Congressional Black Caucus, members of Congress, local political activists and those from around the world would join in a massive protest that the national media had to cover, too. In 1983, President Ronald Reagan signed the MLK Holiday into law and its first Federal observance came three years later.

WHUR-FM was also at the forefront of the Anti-Apartheid Free South Africa Movement in the U.S. On November 21, 1984, Randall Robinson, Executive Director of Trans Africa, Dr. Mary Frances Berry, and Commissioner of the U.S. Commission on Civil Rights, DC Congressman Walter Fauntroy, Georgetown University Law Professor Eleanor Holmes Norton, and a host of political activists convened a sit-in protest at the South African Embassy in Washington, DC and WHUR-FM reporters covered the unpublicized event. The sit-in was to protest the human rights violations of the Apartheid South African government, its brutal suppression of its majority Black population and call for full divestiture of all U.S. economic support of the regime.

The story exploded into the daily news and led to daily arrests of high-profile persons of all races. When the sensation of the story started to wane and news coverage dwindled, WHUR-FM continued its coverage, culminating in Nelson Mandela's release from prison. When South Africa's Police Department harassed our stringer reporter, Subrey Govender, in Durban, South Africa, I registered my concern with the South African Ambassador and told him our press coverage would intensify if they did not cease and desist their harassment.

The next day the South African Police disappeared from in front of his home and left him alone. That's why it is important to have a strong media that is not afraid to deal with despotism. There's a saying that knowledge is power. I say the organized use of knowledge is true power!

Finding God who had been there all the time!

One day I was standing in the center of WHUR'S newsroom, watching my staff busily at work and had a life-changing moment with God. I was at the top of my profession, had real power and influence. Those seeking influence wanted to give me things to impact my news perspective. Money, limos, drugs or anything I wanted, however, I resisted the temptation. This was extremely hard to resist, especially for an *Ex-Incognito Gangster!* I had all the trappings of power, but it was empty. I had a wife and son (our first child) and I loved them dearly. But something was missing.

Then it happened. Just like my father, I let my wife, who had found God, take our son to church, but I wouldn't go. She was attending a small church at the time called the Full Gospel A.M.E. Zion Church that subsequently grew into a mega church. One day I overheard my wife, Gwen, listening to a tape by Pastor John A. Cherry Sr. He was admonishing women not to be at the church every time its doors were open. Rather, they should spend time taking care of their households and husbands, even if he didn't attend church and that they should love their spouses unconditionally. Pastor Cherry also said that if your husband has an issue with you tithing on household money, then tithe off what your husband gives you for you.

I said to myself that I must go and see if this preacher was real!

A child shall lead the way.

My son, Thomas, was glad to see me occasionally go to church with them. When Thomas was about nine years old, he, Gwen and I were in a Sunday service. Pastor Cherry was preaching up a storm and God used him to touch my son's heart. Thomas looked me straight in my eyes and said, "Dad, I'm going to go up and get saved. Are you coming with me?"

I hesitated for what seemed like an hour, finally asking him to wait.

My son politely said, "Excuse me, Dad," and started up the aisle to make his decision for Christ. Gwen started crying tears of joy about what our son had just done. Then God pricked my stony heart. I got up and walked up the aisle to join my son, who waited for me. He took my hand and led me to the altar. I could barely feel my feet touching the ground; however, I knew my legs were moving.

Then everybody in the church heard a shriek and a woman crying loudly saying, "Praise God! Both my husband and son are getting saved!"

I looked back and saw it was my wife, Gwen, making all that noise.

God used my young son to lead me to Him. Years later, I would experience the same role reversal. God would use me to lead my father to Christ.

To God be the Glory!

The emptiness I felt in my life was gone now that I had an authentic relationship with Christ. I stopped cursing, drinking and smoking weed. Despite not being saved when

I married my wife, infidelity was never an issue because I had given up womanizing. I had had my fill of having a lot of women and wanted a relationship with one good virtuous woman. My co-workers at the secular station, WHUR-FM, noticed a change in me, too.

A calling from God to enter All-Time Ministry.

One morning after I had showered and was getting ready to go to work, it happened in my bathroom and it followed me into my bedroom. I had an encounter with God. I heard angels singing and trumpets blaring. I was immersed in a bright light that engulfed my room. I heard an angel speak to me. He told me about myself and God's love for me. God wanted more from me and wanted me to place my trust in Him completely. It was there on my knees that I again, repented of all my sins and the false starts I had had with God. That day I made a Covenant with the Almighty. He wanted me to leave the world for a season. Leave all my power and influence behind, take up my cross and follow Him. That was the day I knew I had to leave WHUR-FM and go into All-Time ministry.

Previously, about a year earlier, God had brought Pastor John A. Cherry Sr. into my life as my Pastor of what was then called the Full Gospel A.M.E. Church in Marlow Heights, Maryland. Years later, it would be re-named From the Heart Church Ministries. Pastor Cherry had been ministering to me about life and how God called him out of a successful construction business to become a pastor. He shared with me some of his early sermons that were only about 15 minutes long. He laughed and said that's all he had to give at the time. But as he got deeper into God's Word, his sermons got better and longer because he had more to say.

Pastor Cherry, who is now a Bishop, saw something in me and told me that God wanted him to get in touch with me and encourage me to go into All-Time ministry. I advised Jim Watkins, my friend, and then General Manager of WHUR-FM, that I was leaving the station to go into All-Time ministry. Initially, he was shocked but gave me a tremendous send-off. Thank you, Jim. Most of my associates and peers in the broadcast industry, who were not Christians, could not comprehend my decision.

Walking away from WHUR-FM at the top of your game and profession was unimaginable. Despite their skepticism, I was the recipient of Mayoral and Congressional Proclamations, received numerous other declarations and well-wishes from WHUR's listeners. This entire period of my life was orchestrated by the Holy Spirit. In my own might, I could not have done it.

Lessons Learned and Thoughts to Ponder:
1. You must make decisions to cease and desist with unproductive activities and then have the courage

and conviction to stick with keeping those crucial choices.

2. When you decide to follow Christ—"Put on the whole armor of God, that you may be able to stand against the wiles of the Devil." (Ephesians 6:11). I also recommend you read, study and internalize Ephesians 6:10-20 to fully understand and use the offensive weaponry of *The Whole Armor of God* when you fight the Devil.

3. If you don't have a plan to succeed, then you plan to fail. Have a plan, but don't be afraid to revise that plan, based on changing market conditions that render your plan ineffective and no longer relevant.

4. Get an education and make it a lifelong process of continual education and sharpening your skillset.

5. After proper preparation for your career path, don't be afraid to Launch out into the deep and let down your nets for a catch. (Luke 5:4). Get off the safety of the shore or familiar circumstances and go deep sea fishing!

6. Decide to work harder than your competition does and become an expert at what you do.

7. Overcome your fears. Fear comes from the Devil and not of God. "For God has not given us a spirit

of fear, but of power and love and of a sound mind." (2 Timothy 1:7).

8. Get a mentor(s)—Look for a person who has been where you want to go and listen to the wisdom they impart, then act on it.

9. Toxicity will drive people away from you, regardless of color, or the validity of how wronged you have been done.

10. God can and will use whomsoever He wills to prick your heart. God used my wife and son to lead me to Christ. My young son grabbed my hand and led me to the altar, which changed my life!

CHAPTER FIVE
All-Time Ministry

Full Gospel A.M.E. Zion Church era—Pastor Cherry, Dr. Myles Munroe, Dr. Fred Price and intro to Mega Ministries

Becoming a Levite in the temple in
All-Time Ministry is not easy!

My first day in All-Time ministry was a day to remember. The years have erased the memory of my formal title at the Full Gospel A.M.E. Zion Church; however, I do remember my responsibilities, which included, Audio Visual, Duplication, Bookstore, Publications and Graphic Department and Music Ministry. I had a lot of people, many of whom were ministers, working under my direction. At that time, I still had to look in the front of the Bible to find various chapters of the Holy Book. On several occasions during my first meetings some of the ministers would say let's read from Haggai or Philemon. I'd say to myself, "WHAT?" I had difficulty finding the Books and they knew it.

This was part of my orientation. I told them I had a relationship with God and explained there was a lot I had to learn about the Bible. I asked for their support, which was given. I, in turn, told them I would make them better managers and we would grow together. All they knew was that I was this guy from the radio, now being their supervisor, having rule over them.

Under the leadership and teachings of Pastor John A. Cherry Sr., I went from a babe in Christ to a full-fledged Christian. Some of his teachings like *Save the Seed,* which is about the role and significance of the male; *Too Close to the Edge,* which is self-explanatory in terms of knowing boundaries and not placing yourself in position to be hurt after being warned not to do so and *Seeking the Lost,* which has a color-coded aspect, dealing with race and religion are all classics.

Pastor Cherry was, and is, an effective preacher and teacher of God's Word. Pastor Cherry also taught me about order in ministry, expanding tape sales and marketing. Drawing on his background in construction and business successes, he developed a program to plant churches across the world. He would secure a building, get it rehabilitated, install AV and support systems, then place a ministerial staff in place to advance the Kingdom. A lot of small churches fail because they can't get past their start-up costs while building up the size of its congregations.

Additionally, I learned from Pastor Cherry to arrive early for church, especially on Sundays, and to walk the church praying for staff, church leadership and the congregation, while all the time rebuking and binding the Devil in Jesus' name. This is something I always did in ministry, way after God had called me to leave All-Time ministry there.

Pastor Cherry also encouraged me to reach out and help smaller ministries that were not functioning at the high level Full Gospel was doing. Deacon Oscar Grant, who was the AV Director at a small church called the First Baptist Church of Glenarden (FBCG) in Landover, Maryland, asked for my assistance.

Years later, FBCG would become a mega church. Deacon Grant needed help in planning tent revivals, how to make his AV Ministry work and increase tape sales. Cassette tapes and DVDs were the dominant format in that day. Little did I know that years later, Deacon Grant would become my friend. He and I would work together in ministry and I would become the AV Director of the First Baptist Church of Glenarden under the leadership of Pastor John K. Jenkins Sr., during my second career in All-Time ministry.

Dr. Miles Munroe

Introduction to mega pastors and ministries worldwide.

Pastor Cherry introduced me to many dynamic mega church ministries and pastors worldwide, such as the late Dr. Myles Munroe of the Bahamas Faith Ministry International in Nassau, Bahamas. Dr. Munroe's teachings and books increased my spiritual knowledge. His praise and worship services would go on sometimes for an hour or more before he preached. This was the first time that I heard Praise and Worship singers utilizing fully-produced tracks with horn and string arrangements, punctuated with a live band and tremendous front of the house (FOH) audio engineering that blew me away. This was way before Motif keyboards and iPads and smartphones were in use for track playback.

For instance, when they ministered to the fully produced track of "Majesty," I felt that I was in Heaven, drenched in sweat and prepared to receive the Word of God like never before. Dr. Monroe would become a life-long friend whom I met with on his many trips to the U.S. He told me to give God my all and don't leave anything in the tank when I die. Dr. Munroe always said the cemetery is full of people who never wrote their book, started a business, or dared to reach their full potential.

He said, "Brother Tom, don't be one of those people, man!"

Charles and Cheryl Phillips

The late Dr. Charles Phillips and his wife Cheryl also taught me about Praise and Worship and music ministry, starting in their ministry in the U.S. Virgin Islands and later when they were on staff at the Full Gospel A.M.E. Zion Church. Through the Phillips' gifts and talents, I perfected using tracks for playback for various artists and meeting their Rider Agreements (contractual equipment and artistic performance requirements).

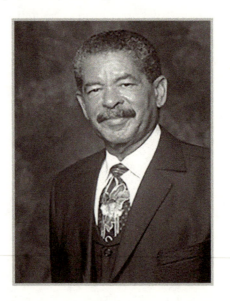

Pastor Cherry also introduced me to Dr. Frederick K. C. Price of the Crenshaw Christian Center in Los Angeles, California, who was, at that time, the biggest Black preacher in America. Years later, when I owned radio stations, Dr. Price always aired his program over my airwaves. It's all about relationships, folks. Same was true with the legendary

Dr. Clay Evans of Chicago, Illinois, who economically supported me with his broadcasts.

Lessons Learned and Thoughts to Ponder:

1. When you decide to follow Christ, and enter All-Time ministry, make sure your decision is sound and you've heard from God—"So likewise, whoever of you does not forsake all that he has cannot be My disciple." (Luke 14:33). I willingly gave up all that I had (status, money, power and influence) and made that decision because I had heard directly from God, who also confirmed it through my wife, Gwen.

2. Have a desire to share your knowledge and make a deposit into God's Kingdom—Help smaller ministries and others who are laboring in God's vineyards.

3. If you don't have a plan to succeed, then you plan to fail. Have a plan, but don't be afraid to revise that plan, based on changing market conditions that render your plan ineffective and no longer relevant.

4. Learn how to operate in the spiritual realm which is different from the secular world. You must develop God's mindset. "For My thoughts are not your thoughts, Nor, are your ways My ways," says the Lord." (Isaiah 55:8).

CHAPTER SIX

Back to the World and Broadcasting

God sent me back into the World to resume my Broadcast career and do great things!

fter years of service and spiritual growth at the Full Gospel A.M.E. Zion Church, God could trust me and therefore, sent me back into the world and the fields of broadcasting and media relations. First, I established a Media Relations firm I called Tom Pope Telecommunications. This provided the seed money I would later use to start a radio network that I would call the TPT Network, an acronym for Tom Pope Telecommunications Network.

My experience and notoriety at WHUR-FM made launching my Media Relations business easy. I secured an office in the National Press Building that was filled with news agencies seeking news and information. I was obliged to provide them with information concerning my clients' propaganda. When the public learned that I was in media relations, clients began to beat a path to my door to write and produce their commercials, develop political campaign strategy, or create effective media campaigns that met their respective needs. I had firsthand contacts in radio, TV, print newspapers and magazines.

Additionally, I was chummy with many of my peers who were now News Directors and Assignment Editors. These are the people who tell and assign reporters what to cover and when, plus determine editorial perspective.

Marion S. Barry, Jr.

Former Mayor Barry needed some political ads created, produced and placed in the media. He remembered my effectiveness at WHUR-FM and gave me contracts for my services on many occasions.

Dr. C. Delores Tucker

Dr. C. Deloris Tucker was embroiled in controversy with Suge Knight over misogynistic lyrics in Rap music that she maintained degraded women. She was under an extreme attack from the Rap and Hip Hop communities and many associated record labels, too. She needed some deep spin control and a proactive media campaign that would better position her for testimony on Capitol Hill and with the news media. I handled that as well as media relations for her Bethune-DuBois Fund organization located in the Watergate complex. Dr. Tucker produced many high-level conferences, banquets and news events that she trusted me to handle. Dr. Tucker was also a tireless worker who began her work day early from her homes in either Washington, DC or Philadelphia, working her staff first thing in the mornings. She would then come to her office in the Watergate complex about midafternoon Eastern time, to do business up until midnight, to deal with West Coast people.

Dr. Tucker and powerful women with
Rosa Parks and Gwen

Dr. C. Deloris Tucker opened the door for me to a number of icons, such as Rosa Parks and Coretta Scott King. Mother Rosa Parks needed work done for her Rosa and Raymond Parks Foundation and numerous media

Rosa Parks

requests for her. When I went back on the air myself, doing a daily radio talk show syndicated into the Detroit, Michigan market, she would listen to me on her radio and would frequently call into my show to comment on topics.

One evening I sat next to her at the Grand Opening of the Detroit Charles H. Wright Museum of African American History. I had a momentary, lecherous relapse telling Rosa Parks, "You're still fine, girl, and look gorgeous tonight!"

She told me in her soft quiet voice, "Stop hitting on me, Tom Pope, or I'm going to tell your wife, Gwen, and get you in a lot of trouble!" We both laughed and I didn't hit on her anymore that night.

Myrlie Evers-Williams   *Rena Evers and Gwen*

Dr. C. Deloris Tucker also talked up my work to Myrlie Evers-Williams. I knew Myrlie through my wife, Gwen, and Myrlie's daughter, Rena, who was, and remains, friends with my wife and me. For years, Myrlie Evers-Williams wanted the man, Byron De La Beckwith, who assassinated her husband, Medgar Evers, brought to justice. Byron De La Beckwith was an avowed White Supremacist and Klansman convicted in 1994 for the 1963 assassination of Civil Rights icon Medgar Evers. For years, this coward successfully evaded justice and thought that he was untouchable. In the end, his conviction was the result of Myrlie's steadfast determination and the media relation's campaign she asked me to wage up until 1994.

My job, along with members of her dedicated team, was to keep this story before the media while she ratcheted up political support for justice. In 1995, Myrlie Evers-Williams also asked me to handle the media relations aspect of her campaign for Chairperson of the NAACP that resulted in her getting the position and pulling the organization out of debt and back to financial solvency.

Tom Pope & Dr. Betty Shabazz

Then came Dr. Betty Shabazz, Malcom X's widow. Dr. Betty was a unique lady. She asked for, and got an appointment, to meet with me in my National Press Building office in downtown DC. She told me she had heard about and seen the type of work I was doing and she wanted me to accept her as a client. If you really got to know Dr. Betty sometimes you knew her language would get a bit "salty" when she was comfortable with you. I still laugh when she would call my house or office and ask Gwen to speak with me. Every now and then she would drop an expletive and then say, "Oops, excuse me, Mr. Pope. I know you're a churchman!"

However, I could never get her to call me by my first name, Tom. As our relationship grew stronger, one evening she told me why she liked my principles, and "You remind me so much of my husband, Malcolm, and you're just like him. That's why I love working with you. Tell Gwen she doesn't have anything to worry about."

Both Gwen and Dr. Betty knew I was always in love with Nancy Wilson, but Nancy and I would never get together.

Dr. Betty also needed personal media relations concerning her foundation in New York and the release of the movie, *Malcolm X*, by Spike Lee to ensure her views were made known. It was magic the night the movie, *Malcom X*, had its New York City debut. Everybody who was anybody in the "Big Apple" and from around the world was there for that glitzy, special night. I can still feel Aretha Franklin's rendition of Donny Hathaway's "Someday We'll All Be Free," as the credits rolled at the end of the movie. The crowd, my wife, Gwen, and I were mesmerized. Dr. Betty also needed me to handle media relations and back-channel communications with Minister Farrakhan regarding one of her daughters being set-up by conspirators, discussing hiring a hitman to assassinate Minister Farrakhan.

Mayor Sharon Pratt Kelly & Tom Pope

Other notable clients included Sharon Pratt Kelly and her campaign to become Mayor of Washington, DC. I first met Mayor Kelly when she was the spokesperson for Pepco, DC's major electricity company, when I was News Director at WHUR. We worked together on numerous projects and she was comfortable with me producing and placing her political campaign ads in the media. This, in addition, to working with her staff on messaging, talking points and debate prep helped her candidacy. She won the campaign and became Mayor of Washington, DC. I continued to provide consul to Mayor Kelly while she was in office.

As stated previously, my media relations office was on one floor of the National Press Building and then I located

D.C. businessman launches major radio network

By Robert N. Taylor

T-P Telecommunications - a Washington, D.C.-based and Black owned media company - this week announced the launching of a *nationally syndicated news and talk network: TPT News, Incorporated.* In so doing, network president and founder Tom Pope, former News Director at WHUR-FM, is directly challenging the domination of the radio news industry by such giants as ABC, CBS and Mutual.

"We are throwing a wide net," says Pope, "because it is time we (Blacks) attempt to shape what is news and what is not." According to the veteran communicator and businessman, TPT News will establish "a new standard in news and information" and "the general public will be the beneficiary."

When the new radio network "goes on line" with 24-hour-a-day programming in February, it will be heard in at least six major metropolitan areas and Pope is projecting that he will have radio stations

in over 100 markets carrying his programming within a year. Locally, TPT News has already signed up an affiliate on the AM band and expects to shortly have an FM affiliate.

"We are clearing (signing up stations to join the network) right now," says Pope while repeating his refrain "we are throwing a wide net" - meaning the network will be signing up not only Black-oriented stations but general market stations as well. Pope found it significant that the network would begin broadcasting in February which is traditionally celebrated as "Black History Month." He explained, "At a time when news and issues are becoming more complex are facing tough economic times forcing them to institute staff reductions. We saw the void and moved to fill it."

The TPT News Network will provide 24-hour national and international news coverage as well as sports, daily talk programs

and public affairs programming. If successful in penetrating 100 markets, the Black-owned network would become one of the major players in the radio industry. The radio industry rating service - Arbitron - lists only 263 radio markets in the entire nation. In

addition to its radio efforts, Pope says his firm has already begun work on the development of some television shows for national syndication.

Pope has already lined up a staff of veteran broadcasters including WHUR News Director Bill Christian who

will serve as TPT News Director and lead anchor; former WRC-AM talk show host Joe Madison who will serve as TPT Director of Syndications as well as host of a talk show on the new network; and noted author, therapist Audrey Chapman who will host a call-

in show on personal relationships. When asked how local residents could support his efforts, Pope confidently advised, "Just hold your information suppliers to a new and higher standard. If you do, we will be able to meet their needs and yours."

Members of the newly launched TPT News Network. From left to right: News Director Bill Christian, Director of Syndications Joe Madison, Chief Financial Officer Ernest Cowan and President and General Manager Tom Pope.

Photo by Charles Ford

the TPT Network several floors above. I gathered some of the best of the best to come and work with me at the TPT Network. Our slogan was "A New Standard in News and Information."

We provided hourly 5 minute newscasts and talk shows. I convinced my former News Editor and News Director at WHUR-FM, Bill Christian, to come and work with me. Joe Madison, now called "The Black Eagle," was our premier syndicated Talk Show Host. Everything was roses. Advertising was rolling in and we were picking up affiliates across the nation, willing to carry our syndicated programming. Despite having outstanding talent and programming, it remains difficult to this day for Black broadcasters to attract sufficient advertising revenue to sustain their operations. A Special Report article published in the November 25—December 2, 1999 issue of the *Washington Business Journal* summarizes our dilemma.

Washington
BUSINESS JOURNAL

VOLUME 18, NUMBER 29 • $1.50   WHERE WASHINGTON CAPITALIZES ON BUSINESS   NOVEMBER 26-DECEMBER 2, 1999

Washington
BUSINESS JOURNAL
S P E C I A L   R E P O R T

'For some reason, Madison Avenue and Fortune 200 companies don't value black listeners,' says Tom Pope, president of PowerNomics Telecom and host of 'The Tom Pope Show.'

ADVERTISING & MARKETING

Unfair share?

Advertisers aren't cashing in on urban radio audiences

By MATTHEW SWIBEL
Staff Reporter

Tom Pope thinks something is shady about radio advertising, and the problem may have everything to do with the color of money.

For many months, Pope has followed a hot trend in local radio and across the country — the everlasting flow of dot-com dollars. The river of cyber-ad revenue has practically saturated airwaves, in some cases drowning out other advertisers.

But just as some say the Potomac divides the Washington area by racial lines, so too may the stream of dot-com dollars.

Web ad revenue appear only to trickle through the front door of the area's popular urban radio stations. But Pope and others say generic advertising dollars follow a similar pattern

Pope recently left WHUR-FM 96.3, which draws the area's third-largest audience among listeners 12 and older, to start a new District-based radio network for African-Americans, PowerNomics Telecom.

"For some reason, Madison Avenue and Fortune 200 companies don't value black listeners," said Pope. "Urban formats have the numbers but don't get same advertising rate."

Washington's black FM stations finished 1-2-3 in October's Arbitron's quarterly rating system. But their revenue ranking among local stations doesn't match up. Radio One-owned WKYS-FM 93.9 has the area's second-largest audience size but it draws smaller billings than at least five other stations.

What gives?

Unlike its news and pop counterparts, many urban stations — especially minority-owned broadcasters — still encounter bias with ad agencies and the companies they represent, some of whom avoid urban in their media buying practices.

And it's more than just hearsay. In January the Federal Communications Commission issued a report showing black and Hispanic radio stations consistently attract less ad revenue than stations that are white-owned or play to a white audience.

It's an issue that radio folk either speak volumes about or don't discuss at all.

The sensitive topic flared up recently when WHUR radio host Tom Joyner organized a grass-roots protest against computer retailer CompUSA, a major advertiser, for allegedly failing to advertise to black consumers.

Joyner — deejay for the area's third-ranked morning show — teamed with BET commentator Travis Smiley to challenge CompUSA's apparent lack of urban radio advertising. During the program, they encouraged listeners to send in CompUSA sales receipts and flex their buying power.

See URBAN, next page

Who's listening?

Duncan American Radio's 1999 annual national report showed area urban stations generally don't draw as many advertising dollars as other stations. The survey takes each station's ranking by market in audience share and divides it into that station's market ranking in advertising revenue. For example, Duncan would place a station that ranks second in audience share and fourth in revenue at 0.5 — 2/4 translated into a decimal. The higher the number, the larger a station's share of advertising revenue is.

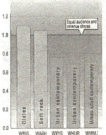

Equal audience and revenue shares

(y-axis: 0.0, 0.2, 0.4, 0.6, 0.8, 1.0, 1.2)

(bars: WBIG — Oldies; WASH — Soft rock; WXYS — Urban contemporary; WHUR — Urban contemporary; WMMJ — Urban adult contemporary)

WASHINGTON BUSINESS JOURNAL

Advertising & Marketing

NOVEMBER 26-DECEMBER 2, 1999

In the air

Radio One isn't the only minority-owned local business interested in making money on radio enterprises. By next year, the local dial may also include music from BET-owned stations and talk from Powernomics Radio Network.

• BET Holdings, the District-based owner of Black Entertainment Television is planning a multi-station buy-out worth as much as $1 billion from Clear Channel Communications. BET wants to enter at least 20 markets and lure more advertising for its media operations aimed at urban black audiences. In order to help pay down debt, BET expects to raise capital by selling shares in its new radio business.

• District-based Powernomics Radio Network was founded in April, after the purchase of Greensboro, N.C.-based Dudley Broadcasting Network. Its 15 affiliates run syndicated programs including urban talk, blues and news commentary. With an estimated audience size of 500,000, it claims to be the fastest-growing urban information and news network in the country.

— *Matthew Swibel*

Urban

continued from preceding page

Ultimately, the brouhaha resulted in a PR nightmare for Dallas-based CompUSA and its CEO, James Halpin, who ended up apologizing on Joyner's morning show. Halpin acknowledged its urban ads accounted for a small piece of their media buy, and promised to hire a black advertising agency by Thanksgiving.

"It's surprising that CompUSA didn't recognize that in many markets — especially Washington — the black middle class is increasing in size," said J.T. Anderson, vice president of Duncan's American Radio. "Given that they understand the targetability of radio, it is hard to figure out how this could happen."

Anderson's company, headquarted in Cincinnati, surveys about 2,000 radio stations to determine how different formats draw different billings sizes.

Specifically, Anderson takes a station's audience share and divides it into revenue. The resulting fraction shows relationship between audience share and revenue share (see chart, page 27).

'Our dollars are not worth less'

Anderson said the problem at urban stations is slowly getting better.

"The truth is that agencies have placed different values on different formats," he said. "Some formats generate relatively high revenue relative to share and some stations underperform. What determines the rate is how much the advertiser is willing to pay for a particular audience."

Michele Williams, station manager at Radio One, understands how this pans out for urban stations.

"Adult contemporary is always a shoo-in," Williams said. "Then the urban stations have to fight it out. It's like the three-fifths compromise [the 1787 Constitutional Convention decision that the federal government would in some situations count 'those bound to service' as three-fifths of a person] — but our dollars are not worth less than anyone else's."

WPGC-FM 95.5 is an exception. Also aimed at the African-American community, the station benefits both from being owned by CBS and because advertisers consider its format broader than that of other urban stations.

Pope said while he worked at WHUR, WTEM, a sports-talk station, and WMAL, a news station, could charge higher advertising rates despite lower ratings.

But Williams keeps a positive outlook.

"I think that hip hop has become more mainstream for people who do not necessarily enjoy hip hop," she said. "Outdoor billboards have a hip-hop flavor — corporations use an urban flavor to get across their messages to the general market."

Advertising on radio is still driven by identifying a target audience.

So if an advertiser wants to target an African-American audience, then the advertiser should be buying on urban radio, said Grace Shiraldi of Silver Spring, an independent buyer of advertising space.

Fitting ads to audience

At the area's No. 2 radio station, WKYS-FM 93.9, a Radio One station, about 80 percent of Radio One listeners are black, nearly 20 percent white, Williams said.

But the station's share of advertising dollars, smaller than that of lower-ranked stations, illustrates that advertisers may not be taking advantage of smart ways to reach an African-American audience.

> **"The truth is that agencies have placed different values on different formats."**
> *J.T. Anderson*
> *Duncan's American Radio*

Shiraldi acknowledged two factors which may contribute to advertisers' avoidance of urban stations:

• Many advertisers who feel they efficiently reach a minority audience with TV perceive urban radio as overkill.

• Only the biggest advertisers have enough money to produce ads for specific markets. As a result, agencies sometimes argue a commercial wouldn't sound right on urban because of its nature.

"If an agency is doing its job correctly, it should always be figuring out who your target audience is," Shiraldi said.

Despite the obstacles, Tom Pope is pressing forward with Powernomics, a $1.1 million radio network carried in 15 markets — all outside D.C. Pope and business partner Brandt Andersen are currently negotiating with various radio power players to syndicate their programming in the area.

"It's not all gloom and doom," he said. "We approach it positively — do you stand outside and curse the darkness?"

Million Man March in Washington, DC

Impact of the Million Man March in Washington, DC

My life was turned upside down, in part, because of my being an avid supporter of the Million Man March (MMM). The Million Man March of October 16, 1995, on the Monument grounds and the steps of the U.S. Congress in Washington, DC had hit. A year before the MMM, Minister Louis Farrakhan, head of the Nation of Islam (NOI), began his national and worldwide promotional campaign. Minister Farrakhan designated Dr. Conrad Worrill of Chicago, Illinois, as the March's main organizer and the Minister also appointed Dr. Ben Chavis as National Director of the MMM.

Dr. Chavis had impeccable civil rights credentials and was one of the Wilmington 10 who had been released from prison in 1980s. The Wilmington 10 consisted of nine young men and a woman, who were wrongfully convicted in 1971 in Wilmington, North Carolina, of arson and conspiracy, and served nearly a decade in jail. They, along with other black residents of Wilmington, North Carolina, were unhappy with the lack of progress in implementing integration and other civil rights reforms legally achieved by the American Civil Rights Movement. Chavis, in later years, would become the Executive Director and CEO of the NAACP. He currently serves as CEO and President of the National Newspaper Publishers Association (NNPA). Dr. Chavis was also active previously in Environmental Justice and Racism Issues having served at the United Church of Christ Commission for Racial Justice.

When I was at WHUR-FM, I regularly interacted with Ben concerning Environmental Justice and Racism Issues. Ben and I had first met through a mutual friend when he was released from prison. We developed a personal relationship that preceded the Million Man March.

We had gathered in my home in DC for a New Year's Eve celebration. I had also previously covered Minister Louis Farrakhan and the Nation of Islam regarding the NOI's Savior's Day observances and its other newsworthy issues.

Mainstream media ignored the upcoming Million Man March story and when coverage was provided, it was generally negative. So, Minister Farrakhan and Dr. Chavis called on the Black media to sensitize the public about the significance of the Million Man March. History reveals that the MMM was not fully embraced by a great many preachers in Black Christian churches as well as a great number of Black organizations and civil rights groups. Plus, most White-led churches with large Black congregations were AWOL, too.

In fact, stark lines of demarcation were drawn and people, in some instances, vehemently started choosing sides. In retrospect, the run-up to the Million Man March marked a period of both extreme divisiveness and unity in the Black community. My TPT Network came under intense pressure to back off from our coverage and support of the March. I met with my staff to explain to them the intensity of the pressure that was put on me to back off. The consensus was that we were a news organization and our critics weren't telling the so-called mainstream media to back off its coverage. We were angry and to the person said, "Let's do it," so we continued our coverage.

Then my advertising began to evaporate because advertisers started receiving threats of boycotts for supporting us. To keep the operation running, I had to rely on my media relations business to underwrite the

Network's payroll, leases and other expenses. This cascaded into several bad financial decisions I made to keep things running and pay the bills.

I'm grateful to God though, for taking me through the Million Man March experience. I achieved some of my highest highs and lowest lows in life during my intense faith walk throughout this tenuous period. At the end of the challenge, God was standing there with His arms open, providing me and my family with a way out.

In 1995, when broadcasters did major live events on the steps of Congress, orders had to be placed weeks in advance for security clearance and phone lines installed by the phone company. Cellcast units were unreliable in a mission critical situation such as the 10-hour Million Man March would be, if you did not have a satellite truck in place. Many of the major news organizations didn't believe the March would happen.

On the day of the Million Man March, many of those ill-prepared news originations had to come to us for the audio feed for radio and television. TPT Network was fully locked in with a complete complement of microphones on the podium, music and crowd as well as lines to and from our studios in the National Press Building so that we could interview notable figures who were not there and take phone calls from our listeners across the world. We also provided a clean pool feed to many in the mainstream media who of course gave us credit for our services.

The stage was set. It was the morning of October 16, 1995, and the Million Man March on the Monument grounds and the steps of the U.S. Congress in Washington, DC had arrived. The TPT Network had the prime location up front on the steps of Congress. It was dark, but you could hear and feel the voices of men stirring and milling around. I also felt the presence of God as something historic was about to unfold. As the sun chased the darkness away and dried up the morning dew, for as far as you could see, there were hundreds of thousands of men, boys and a smattering of women of all ethnicities assembling hours before the event formally began.

Most people assembled were Black, though. But Hispanic, Native American, Asian, Arab and many White people were there, too. Professional athletes, actors and VIPs stood in the crowd like regular people. We also received reports from all three area airports, and especially Washington National, that there was a back-up of private jets seeking hangar and parking space. The high and mighty was there in numbers!

As I reflect on the significance of the Million Man March, it was one of the most powerful and peaceful gatherings of this size I have ever attended. People were courteous to one another and police were well-behaved. DC Mayor Marion S. Barry had personally met with the Federal police and authorities. Plus, Mayor Barry sensitized his Police Chief and the rank and file officers that he wanted them to show restraint and control themselves. There had been rumors and media reports that having a million black men descend upon the Nation's Capital could mean trouble, resulting in potential riots if Minister Farrakhan incited them.

President Bill Clinton and many other national people, who maintained they liked and supported Black people, were suddenly called out of town and were AWOL and MIA. Truth be told that at the MMM, Minister Farrakhan inspired men to take care of their communities, families, register to vote and then actually vote. His closing **Pledge**, that a million men recited in thunderous unison with him at the end of the Million Man March, was an epic closing to an historic event that still resonates today. You could feel the force and power of the million-plus voices!

After the Million Man March, my advertising revenue never recovered. I could no longer make payroll so my employees left because they had families to care for and I had trouble paying my bills. The entire network was sustained by only my wife and me with a few former employees volunteering their time whenever possible.

An angel sent by God delivered me from
the blizzard from Hell.

Just when I thought things couldn't get worse, they did. On Saturday, January 6, 1996, one of the greatest blizzards to hit DC and portions of the Northeast enveloped the Nation's Capital, shutting the city down for days. Gwen, my daughter, Terie and I were experiencing hard times. Fortunately, my son was away and safe at college.

I told Gwen I had to go in and keep the Network going. At first, she pleaded with me not to go but recanted. So, she packed up some food for me to last about 4 days. We prayed and then I trudged out the door into waist high snow, walking from our home in Southeast DC to my office located miles away in downtown DC, several blocks over from the White House. There was an eerie stillness on the frigid, snow covered streets. Icy winds were blowing and, despite my being in DC, it felt like I was on the streets of Chicago in the dead middle of wintertime. The snow was so deep and nothing was moving. After about an hour of trudging for a mile through the snow that was progressively getting deeper and more difficult to navigate, I wanted to give up and turn back. My cell phone had died so I couldn't call for help and nobody could save me anyway, due to the inclement weather and unsurpassable streets. Plus, I knew in my heart I didn't have the strength to make it back because my feet and hands were frozen and my legs were numb. I cried out to God to help me and fell into a snow drift. Then out of nowhere, a man appeared and picked me up.

He told me, "We can make it!"

My strength was renewed as we walked together. He held me up when I faltered, all the while encouraging me onward. We made it to the front of the U.S. Capitol where a single small path had been plowed on the street that ran right past my office in the National Press Building. I turned around to thank the man for encouraging and walking with me, but no one was there. As deep as the snow was, there were no tracks showing where he had gone. Then it dawned on me. That stranger with a soft, positive voice and strength to get two grown men through the snow was an Angel sent by God to help me in my hour of need.

I made it to my office. I slowly thawed myself out, called Gwen and related my experience to her. It had taken me about 6 hours to make the trek from my home to the office and she was concerned for my safety the entire time, but relieved that God had watched over me the whole period.

I also owe a debt of gratitude to the listeners of my TPT Radio Network. They knew we were struggling to keep the Network on the air. They started sending unsolicited donations in to keep us on the air. Listeners especially in my Detroit, Michigan market and my affiliate stations WHPR-FM and TV 33 flew Gwen and me in for a celebration to show us love for our steadfastness and progressive information we disseminated in our broadcasts. Despite my listeners' efforts, eventually I had to make a painful decision and declared bankruptcies for my two companies as well as personally.

Gathering of supporters in Detroit, Michigan

It's one thing to declare bankruptcy when you are a private person; it's an altogether different experience when you're a media personality. The mainstream media, my secured creditors and their slew of attorneys, former employees whom I owed money and the public were there just to see me eviscerated by the Bankruptcy Judge and hounded by a nefarious gang called the "Creditors' Committee" who represented the unsecured creditors. The meanest members of this group made themselves available to the media for the purpose of making public disparaging remarks about my integrity to anyone who would listen.

My source of comfort and guidance was my Bankruptcy Attorney, David Lynn, who remains one of my lawyers to this day. I attempted to shield my family from this entire gut-wrenching affair. It got so bad that I seriously contemplated suicide on several occasions to escape the pain and embarrassment.

Then I thought about the additional hurt I would bring to my family and the loss of my soul and decided this was not the way out. I was extremely depressed. I was operating my businesses under bankruptcy decrees and guidelines and couldn't buy a pen unless I received prior approval from the court.

Don't put limits on God. I prayed for one Black millionaire to financially bail me out from my desperate situation. God sent me two, then two more of varying ethnicities for good measure because He's an equal opportunity Supreme Being!

Once again, I found myself before God stripped of my dignity, broke because of my bankruptcies and self-created sad state of affairs. It was only until I accepted full responsibility for all my bad decisions and repented of my sins did I hear from God. Next, I apologized to my wife and family; friends who had loaned and lost money with me, as well as those close to me that were hurt and embarrassed by my demise. I promised God I would never make these mistakes again. The bankruptcies resulted in the liquidation of all business assets, my home and other personal possessions. We had nothing.

A week before I lost everything and was forced to cease operations, I was in one of studios at my office, praying. Gwen was my receptionist and came into the studio, interrupting my prayer. I had been praying that God would send me a Black millionaire who had deep pockets, long arms and be one who could understand my predicament and help me. She said Dr. Joe L. Dudley Sr. of Dudley Products from Greensboro, North Carolina, was there to see me. He told me that people from around the country had told him of a fellow named Tom Pope located in Washington needed his financial help. Plus, one of his staff members named John Raye, a former TV Anchor for Channel 5 in DC, said he knew and respected me and asked Dr. Dudley to do something. Mr. Dudley was in Washington, DC to attend the Horatio Alger Award on September 23, 1995, event and had decided to talk with me face-to-face.

I explained my predicament and he said it didn't scare him. He said he would return with his wife, Dr. Eunice Dudley, CFO of Dudley Products. I had been praying for one Black millionaire and God sent me two! Lesson learned is don't limit God. The Dudleys, Gwen and I met in the studio. The upside to my bankruptcies was that I had all my paper work in order such as business plans, financial statements, projections, assets, etc. We poured over the documents and Mr. Dudley concluded that he could not save my Network. If he did try, I would probably pull him into financial disaster too. My heart sank. Then he said, Tom and Gwen, leave all of this behind and we'll start a new radio Network and you can name it whatever you want. I told him it would be the Dudley Broadcasting Network.

He said, "I have many pieces of property and we'll build you a new station and show you how to make it profitable." He also said, "Eunice and I will relocate you and your family to the Greensboro, North Carolina, area and give you a fresh start and put you in a house. We just ask that you and Gwen take a break first and allow yourselves time to heal."

Mr. Dudley further stated that their travel agency would book us flights to one of their Florida homes for some sunshine and serious R&R if we chose to do so.

God had moved on the Dudley's hearts to encourage us and re-build our self-esteem. Mrs. Dudley showed me how to manage money, work a budget according to my business plan, and keep my books properly. Mr. Dudley expanded my business acumen and opened my mind to a new way of thinking. He introduced me to a number of motivational books and self-help authors such as Napoleon Hill and his books *The Law of Success, Positive Mental Attitude, Think and Grow Rich*, Dr. Robert Collier's *Secret of the Ages* and *Riches Within Your Reach* along with a variety of other self-help books as well as the *Holy Bible*.

Most mornings, Mr. Dudley would take walks with the three key male members of his staff. Those men were John

Raye, Dr. Willie Bailey and me. We would discuss topical events of the day, report on the progress of our various departments and whatever book all of us were reading at the time. We would also have reading sessions, while not talking to each other that would last 3 - 4 hours, which is not easy to do. This built up my mental discipline and concentration abilities that I had never experienced before. Mr. Dudley decided to write his autobiographical book called *Walking by Faith: I Am I Can & I Will*. He asked John Raye, Dr. Willie Bailey and myself to assist him in organizing and writing his book.

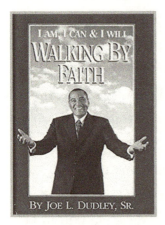

Walking by Faith is the story of how Mr. Dudley overcame poverty, a speech impediment and being branded a slow-learner, to launch a home-based health and beauty product manufacturing business with his wife, Eunice, and growing it into a global empire. Here are Mr. Dudley's own words; "Who could ever have guessed? We started mixing products in our kitchen. Now we have grown to have impact on economic and business development on an international level. Who could have guessed? Certainly not I. My life goes to show that there is no limit to how far just one good idea can take a person. I pray that, in some small way, this book, *Walking by Faith*, will add a new dimension to your life. Additionally, I hope it will cause you to feel that God has a purpose for your life. I want you to be excited about uncovering that purpose. There is something very special in store for you if only you will believe, in faith, that all things are possible."

Thank you, Mr. and Mrs. Dudley, for loving and caring for me and my family while bringing restoration to us at a time when we were bruised and broken!

I also want to to extend a deep debt of gratitude to Pastor Michael A. Ellerbe, Founder and Senior Pastor of the New Beginnings Full Gospel Ministries in High Point, North Carolina. During our time in the Greensboro area he was our pastor who guided Gwen and myself from a period of hurt and led us into spiritual restoration. Thank you Pastor and First Lady Janice Ellerbe for loving us.

Another Black millionaire, whom I developed a personal relationship with, was the late Don Barden of Detroit, Michigan. Mr. Barden owned casinos in Indiana, Mississippi and Las Vegas, Nevada. He also owned an automotive plant in Namibia, Southwest Africa that retrofitted General Motors manufactured vehicles to meet local standards. Don Barden got his start working on an automotive assembly line in Lorain, Ohio, which is about 40 miles from Sandusky, Ohio. He worked his way to Detroit, Michigan, eventually owning Detroit's cable TV franchise and made his first money in broadcasting.

We were kindred spirits from Ohio who both loved broadcasting. Don Barden knew the significance of Black ownership of radio and television and the need to economically support the industry through regular advertising. I still remember him mentoring me in his spacious office at the top of the iconic GM Renaissance Center Building in Detroit that had a panoramic view of the city, the Detroit River and the Canadian city of Windsor.

During those sessions, he taught me how to build organizations, imparted his philosophy about money and how to leverage resources to your advantage. God bless Don Barden!

Back to Mr. and Mrs. Dudley of Dudley Products and the Dudley Broadcasting Network. When I first came to the Dudleys, Mr. Dudley told me we both would know when it's time for me to leave. He and his wife, Eunice, had built Gwen and I back up mentally, spiritually and financially. He also personally protected me from one extremely bad creditor in North Carolina who falsely accused me of owing him money. Gwen and I both healed and grew at Dudley Products. Mr. Dudley told me before I left, he wanted me to write them a check and pay for the broadcast equipment they purchased for us. I was proud to deliver a Cashier's Check for the agreed upon purchase price!

I was determined to resurrect my
Broadcasting career in Washington, DC.

Next up, Gwen and I continued our rise from self-created ashes like a phoenix and made our triumphant return to Washington, DC. I had some people who had previously threatened me saying, "Don't come back to DC or we'll get you!"

I introduced them to the old Gangster side of Tom Pope and met iron with iron saying, "I'm Back. I Ain't Going Nowhere and Bring It!"

Opposition to my returning to DC soon melted away.

Before I left Dudley Products, I had developed a relationship over the years with Dr. Claud Anderson. Claud and his wife Joann are true friends of Gwen and mine. It was through Dr. Anderson's books and lectures I gained a better insight into the issue of race in America, how we got into this situation and how do we resolve it. Allow me to provide you with some background on him.

Dr. Claud Anderson is an author, business person and lecturer. He is president of PowerNomics® Corporation of America, Inc. (PCAI). His concept of PowerNomics® is the package of principles and strategies he developed to explain the concept of race and to offer a guide for Black America to become a more economically and politically competitive group in America.

Dr. Anderson's book, *PowerNomics: The National Plan to Empower Black America*, incorporates and reflects his past experiences, his academic research, business experience, both as an owner and a capital provider. He has held the highest positions in federal and state government and politics. He was State Coordinator of Education for Florida under Governor Reuben Askew during the tumultuous period of the 1970s. After successfully creating social reform projects in Florida and leading President Jimmy Carter's Florida campaign to a win in the state, Carter appointed Anderson as the Federal Co-Chairman for a Commission of Governors in the southeast states. In that position (rank of assistant secretary in the U.S. Department of Commerce), he chaired the commission, funded and directed economic development projects for the governors in those states. The projects he funded created jobs and businesses in those states. As executive director of two economic development corporations for the city of Miami, Florida, he oversaw funding of more than 30 businesses. Although he has been a political independent for many years, he was a major planner and coordinator for the 1988 Democratic Convention in Atlanta and has taught at all levels of education.

Dr. Anderson is also president of The Harvest Institute, a nationally recognized think tank that does research, policy development, education and advocacy to increase the self-sufficiency of Black America. I'm proud to be a member of the Board of Directors for The Harvest Institute. Dr. Anderson's books, *Black Labor, White Wealth: A Search for Power and Economic Justice* and *PowerNomics: The National Plan*, are the foundation for Harvest Institute programs.

His latest book puts the issue of race into perspective and I strongly recommend you get a copy for your own edification. Claud's wife, Joann, and my company Tom Pope Media collaborated on the following Press Release:

The book is entitled ***A Black History Reader: 101 Questions You Never Thought to Ask*** provides answers and solutions to how and why Black people have been consigned to the lowest level of America's ranking order of social and economic acceptability.

Today, America finds itself embroiled in issues of the Confederacy, slavery, immigration and a myriad of issues based on race and racism. Why is race such an enduring problem? How is it that Blacks are always on the bottom? How is it that even the Black Civil Rights era produced more gains for other class groups than the intended beneficiaries, Blacks? Is there any hope that the issue of race will ever be resolved? *A Black History Reader: 101 Questions You Never Thought to Ask* is Dr. Claud Anderson's fifth installment in an impactful series of books designed to deconstruct the topic of race and offer guidance toward self-sufficiency to Blacks around the world. The three-fold purpose of *A Black History Reader: 101 Questions You Never Thought to Ask* is to:

1. Present its reader with America's Constitution-based social construct that historically established and fixed the racial relationship between Blacks and Whites.
2. Declare the exceptionality of the descendants of slaves in America, their unique and substantive contributions to the development to this country and their maltreatment by all segments of this society.
3. Highlight the acute need in Black America for long-overdue reparations based on the exceptionality of the way their group has been viewed and treated.

Dr. Claud Anderson's Other Books:

1. *Black Labor, White Wealth*—The Search for Power and Economic Justice.
2. *PowerNomics*—The National Plan to Empower Black America.
3. *Dirty Little Secrets* about Black History,

Its Heroes and Other Troublemakers.

4. ***More Dirty Little Secrets*** about Black History, Its Heroes and Other Troublemakers, Vol. II.

Powernomics Radio Network

A New Standard in News and Information

With this backdrop, Claud and I formed the Powernomics Radio Network (PRN) in Washington, DC, with offices located in the Florida Avenue Baptist Church, whose Pastor is Dr. Earl D. Trent Jr. These gentlemen, along with other members of the Harvest Institute, allowed me to resume the mission of my prior radio networks. We were also joined by Dr. Walter P. Lomax Jr. of Philadelphia, Pennsylvania, who made his fortune as a medical practitioner that established Lomax Health Systems, Inc., a management company contracting exclusively on health care recruiting of physicians in the Philadelphia area. These individuals, along with Dr. Dudley of Dudley Products and Casino magnate, Don

Barden, were my brain trust and financial backers. In addition, radio and TV station owner Mr. R.J. Watkins of Detroit, Michigan, radio station group owner and Attorney Percy Squire of Columbus, Ohio, radio station owner, Mr. Richard Weaver Bey of Hartford, Connecticut, listeners and numerous national and local political activists from across the country, supported the Powernomics Radio Network.

Powernomics Radio Network programming featured the daily four-hour Tom Pope Talk Show and regular commentary from Dr. Claud Anderson. My wife, Gwen, served as my Producer and booked many high-profile guests, authors along with national and local authors of all races and creeds. Guests included, Mother Rosa Parks, Dr. Betty Shabazz, Dr. Rosie Milligan, Jimmy Dean (the sausage man), major recording artists, best-selling authors, Vivica Fox, Detroit Mayor Kwame Kilpatrick, Minister Louis Farrakhan, Tom Joyner, Tavis Smiley, Michael Baisden, Dr. John Henrik Clarke, Dr. Ben Carson, Dr. Frances Cress Welsing, Neely Fuller Jr., Dr. Charles S. Finch, timely news topics, national and local activists.

Lessons Learned and Thoughts to Ponder:

1. Once in All-Time ministry—Continue to listen to God's voice and directions.

2. God will prepare you for where He wants you to go. My journey took me back into the secular world so He could use me there.

3. You must be a Christian 24/7. Don't be guilty of hiding your faith in secular settings, on the job, or around friends and family?

4. Don't be intimidated by powerful people—they have the same fears and desires you have. In fact, they may have more challenges and hang-ups than you because of their notoriety.

5. When you give your word to someone, honor it.

6. Become a voracious reader of various types of books that will help you grow and stimulate your way of thinking.

    a. Motivational books and self-help authors such as Napoleon Hill and his books, *The Law of Success, Positive Mental Attitude, Think and Grow Rich,* Dr. Robert Collier's *Secret of the Ages* and *Riches Within Your Reach.*

    b. *The Holy Bible.*

    c. *Walking by Faith* by Dr. Joe L. Dudley Sr.

    d. Dr. Claud Anderson's books; *Black Labor; White Wealth –The Search for Power and Economic Justice, PowerNomics—The National Plan to Empower Black America, Dirty Little Secrets about Black History, Its Heroes and Other Troublemakers* and *A Black History Reader: 101 Questions You Never Thought to Ask.*

CHAPTER SEVEN

Return to All-Time Ministry

Called back into All-Time ministry to
build up people and systems in God's Kingdom.

Between the years 2003—2005, God starting tugging on my heart to return to All-Time Ministry. This was something I did **NOT** want to hear because I had finally put it all together and was having too much fun all over the nation and world. People were flying me all over the country; I was back riding in limousines, staying at 5 Star hotels and given all kinds of perks. I was the captain of my ship and master of my own destiny. It was the good life and, as they say, it was, "Deja vu all over again!" However, in 2004, the tugging from God intensified.

I had joined First Baptist Church of Glenarden (FBCG) in the year 1990 and initially was not very active in ministry. Through my TPT Radio Network and, as a volunteer, I started editing FBCG's radio broadcast as a means of giving back to God for all he had done for me. Later in about 2004, I started volunteering at First Baptist as a writer and editor. Then when President Bush visited First Baptist Church of Glenarden on Martin Luther King Jr. day to speak, it set off a firestorm in the Black media.

Pastor Jenkins was being denigrated daily in the media, especially on the Tom Joyner Morning Show, along with commentary from Tavis Smiley, for allowing the Presidential visit on MLK Day, saying a Black church, FBCG, was being exploited for political purposes. Nobody wanted to hear that if the President of the United States asks to come visit you, you don't turn him down out of respect for his Office because he is the President. This visit occurred at the same time First Baptist had an increased demand for writers and editors because of the tremendous growth of the ministry.

Mega ministries generate a lot official letters, reports and correspondence. FBCG needed to handle this crisis, but had no formal Public Relations Department in place at that time. Subsequently, the Media Relations Ministry was birthed after the crisis, which was the precursor of FBCG's current Marketing & Public Relations Department. Good PR, or Media Relations, is a necessity during a crisis. Don Barden had told and showed me how to leverage resources and influence to my advantage.

Since I knew everybody who was beating up on Pastor Jenkins, it was not difficult to quietly work toward a positive resolution of the controversy. This coupled with new stories and topics raised in the rapidly changing ongoing news cycle diminished the significance of the controversy. First, I started on my own talk show, putting the Bush visit in perspective. Part of what I love about Pastor Jenkins is that he **NEVER** asked me to do it. God moved on my heart to do it because I had the power and influence to bring about positive change.

The benefit of being obedient to God was that I met a woman named Iris Skinner who served with me as the Vice President of the Media Relations Ministry. Iris would eventually become the first Director of Marketing & Public Relations at First Baptist. When we first met, we immediately became close associates, and then our relationship quickly blossomed into friendship. My wife, Gwen, and Iris' husband, Calvin, understood our relationship and both blessed our close friendship and neither of them was jealous of it.

I know that I'm a great writer, however, Iris could write circles around me when it came to Annual Reports, press releases, formal technical reports, graphics, layouts and printing. My forte is spin control, radio and TV productions, media plans, media purchases and oral communications. We complemented each other.

The day Iris was called home to be with the Lord is the day my heart broke. And the day of her Homegoing Celebration service there was not a dry eye in the church.

In fact, I still hurt from her death to this very day because Iris was, and remains, my buddy. I look back on the days when she and I would have differences or arguments and not be speaking with one another. She would call Gwen and tell her she was not speaking with me but ask her to give me a message. I would reciprocate with Calvin. She would also drop a dime on me to Gwen in a minute if she saw me not eating the right types of food and would bring me healthy snacks to work on a regular basis. I can still hear Iris' voice. She spoke in a rapid-fire cadence and her words would hit you like bullets coming from an automatic weapon. Make her mad and she would do a verbal drive-by on you! My sincere desire is to see Iris again when the Lord calls me home, however, I'm not in a hurry for that to happen because of my unfinished business here on earth.

In the years 2004—2005, my wife Gwen confirmed what God had been telling me and that was it was time for me to return to All-Time ministry. Then the late Elder Grier of the First Baptist Church of Glenarden started heavily recruiting me to come onboard as staff because he felt my skillset was needed. Then he brought God into the situation. Then Elder Terry, who was a Deacon at the time, whom I had consulted with on the AV aspect of construction on FBCG's Ministry Center, said the church could use my skills. Then I heard from the late Deacon Oscar Grant who told me the same thing based on my consultations with him about AV and other issues when I was on staff at the Full Gospel A.M.E. Zion Church. Then I finally heard from Pastor Jenkins who wanted me to come on staff and oversee the AV construction aspect of the new Worship Center and prepare his staff and volunteers for the transition. Jac Cooney who was serving as the part-time AV Director and whose opinion Pastor Jenkins respects said after my job interview, "Tom, the job is yours."

After hearing from God and those pillars of the church, I formerly came onboard as staff at the First Baptist Church of Glenarden in November 2005.

First Baptist is my home church. And under the teachings of Pastor John K. Jenkins Sr., I have experienced tremendous spiritual growth. He has taught me so much through his integrity in business, adroit organizational skills and his being a boss that lets you do your job and provides you with the resources to be successful. Once I gained his trust, he gave me the freedom to walk in the gifts God had blessed me with. Here's a thumbnail sketch, under the leadership of Pastor Jenkins, my responsibilities and accomplishments serving as Director of the Audio-Visual Department for the First Baptist Church of Glenarden:

From 2005—2016 Director of the Audio-Visual Department of the First Baptist Church of Glenarden which has five divisions: Audio, Video, AV Services, Production and Editing.

Major responsibilities:

1. Direct the workflow of 13 staff members and over 150 volunteers and contractors.

2. Created and Chief Editor of FBCG News and copy and responsible for producing FBCG's Radio Broadcasts, Sunday Services, Bible Study, Web Stream, 24/7 Monitors and technical production of all major events.

3. Place advertising buys for Radio & TV, in addition to developing associated copy and audio-visual concepts.

4. Oversee the acquisition of AV equipment and preventive maintenance of all AV equipment on our various campuses.

5. Provide strategic AV plans and budgets for the new Family Life Center and other long-term projects and facility buildouts.

Lessons Learned and Thoughts to Ponder:

1. Sometimes God will have you repeat a lesson or mission and test your faith during the process. The second time around decision to re-enter All-Time ministry was harder to make. Then God put me in remembrance of His Word—"So likewise, whoever

of you does not forsake all that he has cannot be My disciple." (Luke 14:33).

2. Regardless whether you are in All-Time or volunteer ministry, there are seasons of your service.

3. During my service at the First Baptist Church of Glenarden, God used all the gifts He had given me—Use what you've got.

   a. I utilized journalistic, media relations skills, management and strategic long-range planning abilities, creativity, technical and construction knowledge.

4. Learned to study the Bible better and develop a kinder heart!

CHAPTER EIGHT

New Beginnings, New Ministry and New Company

Transitions—back into the world with a new assignment from God!

After 11 years of faithful service at the First Baptist Church of Glenarden, it was time for me to retire, rest and prepare for the next chapter in my work to advance God's Kingdom. I had started preparing for my departure two years out before I left. At my retirement party celebration, Jac Cooney, who was my predecessor as AV Director at FBCG, reminded me, saying, "Tom, you told me a year ago that this would be your last year at FBCG and man, you kept your word!"

I always consult with my wife, Gwen, and encourage you to talk with your spouse before making major decisions. We had gone on a cruise about 3 or 4 months before my official retirement on December 31, 2016, and both agreed as we sat on our outside cabin balcony of the ship overlooking the pristine aqua-colored Caribbean waters that my time was up at FBCG. I had discussed my going forward plans with Gwen the year before I left the First Baptist Church of Glenarden that God had blessed. I formed my new company called Tom Pope Media.

As word had gotten around the country that I had retired from the First Baptist Church of Glenarden, job opportunities and offers started pouring in. I respectfully declined the generous offers because I was not looking for a job.

January 1—July 1, 2017, I rested, took time to fast, spent time reading my Bible, listening to the voice of God and basically slept my way through most of January 2017. I also reflected on my entire life experiences while objectively examining my successes and failures. After an extensive review, I came to some conclusions about what I would do with the second half of my life. The first half was spent chasing success, fame, fortune, career goals and raising a family. So, I spent February through July 2017, pondering what my significance would be that God revealed to me. It's important to be still and wait on the Lord to lead and direct your path. I went through this process before having read Bob Buford's book called *Half Time - Moving From Success to Significance.* If you are at the mid-life or half time portion of your life, I strongly recommend you read Bob Buford's book that will guide you through the process so you won't be in a period of crisis and indecision. If you are a proactive person, I suggest you read the book while in your

30s or 40s. I guarantee it will help prepare you to deal with the ebb and flow of life.

As I stated previously I was not looking for job that would restrict my freedom. Rather, God's plan for my life is for me to help pastors, ministries (large and small) and select secular businesses to advance His Kingdom. Here's a brief overview of Tom Pope Media that God has blessed me with to advance His Kingdom.

TomPopeMedia

Tom Pope Media Overview

Tom Pope currently serves as the CEO of Tom Pope Media (TPM), a multi-media company. The Praise Power Network, a web-based Gospel radio network, is a subsidiary of TPM. TPM specializes in various forms of media including broadcast, editorial services, major corporate event planning, advertising & media placement, marketing & public relations and AV systems installation. TPM's principles have a wealth of media experience covering all the disciplines our organization provides. Our list of award-winning associates and support firms are at the top of their respective games and can handle big and small events in the Washington, DC area and around the nation. We serve from the U.S Monument grounds, Federal facilities, to large and small conference and convention centers, major concert production to specializing in big and small church events and productions.

We're a "One Stop Shop," so there is no need for you to run around looking for the right team to handle your needs.

As I wind down my life story called, ***From Incognito Gangster to God: An American Story of Redemption and Restoration,*** I hope that I have encouraged you to achieve your dreams and seek a personal relationship with God. Regardless where you begin in life, you can overcome any disadvantages and become successful by keeping your heart and eyes on Christ. I also want to refer you to a message entitled, *"Don't Despise Humble Beginnings That Shape Your Destiny,"* preached by one of my clients who have become a friend and supporter. His name is Pastor Alonzo Walker, the senior pastor of Bethel Deliverance Outreach Ministries located in Upper Marlboro, Maryland.

Life experiences that shaped my destiny
made me the man I am today.

Lessons I learned participating in organized athletic teams at its highest levels aided me in building winning teams and organizations throughout my professional career. I always demanded excellence of myself first and would never ask any of my subordinates to do a task I was not willing to do. Next, everybody on my team was required to put forth a maximum effort. In areas where they might lack expertise, I made sure they received training that would bring them up. If that didn't work, then they had to find a new team where mediocrity was accepted.

Over the years many have misunderstood my actions, thinking I was too hard or mean-spirited. At WHUR-FM behind my back certain staff members rightfully so, called me either Darth Vader, Lord Vader or "Massa" Pope before my encounter with God. In All-Time Ministry, only the slackards said I was too demanding or mean. Nothing is further from the truth. I have a "Champion's" heart instilled in me from my early youth and was taught never to settle for mediocrity or being second best! I don't entertain mediocrity well and have no room for it on my team or in my space.

At the outset of my book, I told you that I'm a product of the **Baby Boomer** generation who was destined to become an Alpha Male. Over the course of my career, I have always been the guy in charge and quite frankly, I relish the role. This, despite being born Black and poor in a time of extreme racism in America (1948). Plus, I was a chronic stutterer who could not speak very well having verbal communicative challenges. I hated it when people would complete sentences for me, or slap me on my back as if it would magically help get my disjointed words out. And when it came my turn to read aloud in class, I experienced anxiety attacks out of fear and loathing because some of the other kids would always openly laugh at me stuttering so badly. I was thoroughly embarrassed.

Down but not out for the count!

Most of my early life, we did not have running water in our home, which was a small trailer. As a paperboy, I had to literally fight most every day while running a gauntlet of mean-spirited dogs for whom I was their featured afternoon entertainment and endure an unending supply of malicious White and Black people, just to deliver my newspapers to earn money to help pay for my school clothes. Plus, I hustled up odd jobs to make additional money. Along the way, I developed an appetite for violence and loved to fight and beat down those people who used to bully me.

I also had to overcome racism in school because there weren't many Black kids in my elementary classes. Not all my teachers were racist; however, despite the racism which existed, I did well on standardized tests so I still received good grades. I grew up hating White people most of my life because of what they had and what I didn't.

So, I studied them up close and learned their culture. After intimate exposure in their homes, businesses and through athletics, my views began to change and so did my heart. In fact, I developed life-long relationships with Whites I grew up with that exist today. And I now have many wholesome relationships with Whites and other ethnic groups with whom I conduct business every day. I challenge you to get out of your comfort zone and develop relationships with people who do not look or think like you.

Yes, I found God at an early age, then fell away from him and became an ***Incognito Gangster***, who concealed my true inner self, which was a chauvinistic, cold-hearted, ruthless criminal and vicious thug for most of my life. That is, until God gave me the love of my life, my wife, Gwen, whom He used to softened my heart and mind. He blessed our union with two children, in addition to a niece and nephew we helped raise, plus, He has given us a growing number of grandchildren, too.

"I can do all things through Christ who strengthens me."
– Philippians 4:13

If someone like me can change and rise above his humble beginnings, you can, too. Not in my wildest dreams, I would ever think I'd meet, know and have relationships with so many great people who have literally changed the course of the world. Who would have thought that a chronic stutterer would become a radio and TV announcer, making his living through public speaking? My grandparents, parents and family members, some teachers, friends and other broadcasters had faith in me and never discouraged me from achieving my dreams and goals.

Most importantly, God had faith in me! He walked alongside of me and sometimes carried me on His mighty, broad shoulders. I now realize I should have been killed many times over suffering a violent death because of my lifestyle and poor choices, however, God's angels always protected me, in spite of me.

Folks, let me serve notice, that after achieving so much success in the first half of my life, I'm just getting started on a new journey. In the second half of my life, I'm now moving toward major significance and a future pregnant with possibilities. My final thought and major lesson I've learned during my years on earth is don't limit God's capabilities. To God be the Glory!

Lessons Learned & Thoughts to Ponder:

1. It pays to follow God!
2. Love your spouse and family!
3. Have a plan, then work the plan!
4. Dare to dream Big!
5. Develop a "Champion's" heart and never settle for mediocrity, or being second best!
6. Nobody gets ahead all by himself or herself. Make friends and be a friend to someone!
7. It doesn't matter where you start from in life; you have the power and ability to determine your own outcome through Christ!

8. Learn how to strategically move from success to significance in life!
9. Keep God first in your life!

ABOUT THE AUTHOR

Tom Pope currently serves as the CEO of Tom Pope Media (TPM), a multi-media company. He is also the founder of the Praise Power Network, a web-based Gospel radio network, which is a subsidiary of TPM. TPM specializes in various forms of media, including broadcast, editorial services, major corporate event planning, advertising and media placement, marketing and public relations and AV systems installation. TPM has an impressive list of current and past clients.

From 2005 to 2016, during a period of major technological and broadcast growth, Tom Pope served as Director of the Audio-Visual Department of a megachurch, the First Baptist Church of Glenarden located in suburban Maryland near Washington, DC.